DR. MARTENS
THE STORY OF AN ICON

MARTIN ROACH

CW00921323

DR. MARTENS
THE STORY
OF AN ICON

MARTIN ROACH

Chrysalis
Impact

First published in 2003 by Chrysalis Impact
An imprint of Chrysalis Books plc
The Chrysalis Building, Bramley Road, London, W10 6SP,
United Kingdom

A member of **Chrysalis** Books plc
© 2003 Chrysalis Books plc

ISBN 1 84411 011 7

Text © Martin Roach
Volume © Chrysalis Books plc 2003

All rights reserved. No part of this book may be reproduced,
stored in a retrieval system, or transmitted in any form or by any
means, electronic, mechanical, photocopying, recording or
otherwise, without the prior permission in writing of Chrysalis
Books PLC.

Commissioning editors: Will Steeds, Chris Stone
Project editor: Laura Ward
Photography: Neil Sutherland, Michael Wicks
Designed by Grade Design Consultants, London
Colour reproduction: Anorax Imaging
Printed and bound in Italy

The editors would like to thank Charlotte Hagan at AirWair for
sharing her extensive knowledge of Dr. Martens, 'the brand', and
for her friendly support and advice.

AirWair, the AirWair Ball and Airwair with Bouncing Soles are
registered trademarks of R Griggs Group Ltd and its
subsidiaries. DR. MARTENS, DOC MARTENS AND DM's are
registered trademarks used under licence.

The depiction or description of any individual or group does not
constitute an endorsement of, or affiliation with AirWair
International Limited or Dr. Martens brand products. The use of
text, graphic or photographic material herein does not constitute
an endorsement or affiliation of the creator of the material with
AirWair International Limited or Dr. Martens brand products.

The content, views and opinions expressed herein do not
necessarily reflect those of AirWair International Limited, its
employees or affiliates, or the Dr. Martens brand. The inclusion of
material herein does not constitute a commercial endorsement
by AirWair International Limited, its employees or affiliates, or
the Dr. Martens brand and shall not be used in any manner to
suggest such endorsement. This is not an official book.

Dedicated to Gary Pettet – 'Alroit, mate'

Martin Roach

Stephen Griggs (left) and his father Max.

Martin Roach is the author of more than 80 books on music, film, celebrity and youth culture. Described by *Melody Maker* as '*the* biographer of youth culture and music' and by *Record Collector* as 'a publishing prodigy', Roach also runs two publishing houses, Independent Music Press and I.M.P. Fiction. To date, his books have amassed global sales in excess of two million copies.
To contact him, visit www.impbooks.com

The current Vice Chairman of Dr. Martens, Stephen Griggs, is the fifth generation of Griggs to run the company. Stephen was born in 1961 – the year after the 1460 was launched – and for the first eleven years of his life lived next door to the company headquarters. His old bedroom is now an AirWair office. He left school aged sixteen, and became a trainee accountant, before spending a year studying shoemaking at Wellingborough Technical College. He joined his father's company at the age of 21, and his first task – sticking felt pads into the soles of the boots – lasted six months. He took over as Group Chairman in 1993 and became Vice Chairman in 2002. Max Griggs (pictured above, right) is the current President of AirWair.

Contents

Foreword

Dr. Martens mean something. The core of their appeal lies in their extraordinary heritage and deep association with youth culture. This is not the sort of association that comes from advertising and marketing ploys, but a genuine connection, born out of the youth of each era adopting the boot as their own. Like Levi's, Dr. Martens were the choice of the younger generation long before they were advertised. Converse have a similar connection, with pictures of a dead Kurt Cobain wearing the trainers, yet DM's go back much further than that.

This heritage is not a millstone – on the contrary, it is a unique facet.

Dr. Martens do not reflect youth culture, they are a part of it. Look at the pictures in this book, read the words. The boots are on the feet of countless youth movements, and that means so much. Even if a youngster hasn't yet come across Dr. Martens, show him or her any of these images, get them to soak up these tales, and they will immediately recognize the significance.

This brand means an awful lot to me personally, because Dr. Martens played an integral role in the growth of Red Or Dead. It is also no secret that I have been intimately involved with Dr. Martens over the years and have a genuine fondness for both the brand and the Griggs family. They are nice, 'human' people in an industry where these qualities are often in short supply.

DM's will always be with us. The brand, like any other, will have its highs and lows. But because of its incredible, rich heritage, it will always be there, bubbling underneath.

Wayne Hemingway
Co-founder of Red Or Dead
March 2003

Preface

Few brands can boast the cultural potency and rich heritage in which each new pair of Dr. Martens boots is steeped.

Since its inception in 1960, the working-man's boot has won a diverse allegiance from an incredible array of subcultures, being fiercely championed by skinheads, punks, psychobillies, grebos, mods and many others. Each generation has in turn recycled and reignited the boot's currency in the youth market, heaping yet more history on its simple shape, such that it has now successfully seeped into every corner and crevice of underground life.

For years I was fascinated by this story. My own first pair of DM's came shamefully late in life, at the age of eighteen. I just wasn't cool enough to wear them before that. When I was at school, I recall my mother telling me that I couldn't have a pair because they were 'for yobbos'. At that point in their evolution, this was often true. Monkey boots were an option, but I steered clear of both. A great friend of mine, Darren Neath, had a pair of Dr. Martens and I thought it was the coolest thing out. So long as he didn't kick me up the arse with them. We used to play a game in the school fields called British Bulldog. A handful of unfortunates stood at one end of the pitch, with a melee of Dr. Martens-clad classmates in the centre, lying in wait. The object of the game was to get to the other side of the pitch without being cut down by the scything sweep of eight-hole DM's. I always lost, sliced to the floor with bruised shins and watering eyes. Darren never lost. He had his DM's.

So for me Dr. Martens represented this strange combination of feared weapon and envied possession. It was only when I left school, and started learning more about social history and youth culture, that it became apparent that there was so much more to the 1460 than cherished yet – it has to be admitted – painful childhood memories.

Along with a close colleague, Gary Pettet, I started researching the brand and eventually, in 1999, we released a corporate history of the boot to celebrate its 40th anniversary. Between us, we turned up 40,000 pictures featuring Dr. Martens, and also interviewed countless figures from music and youth culture who loved the brand. The warmth and passion with which this project was met made me think there was still far more to discover.

So I started researching again, delving further into the brand's astonishing history, looking at the boot in the context of each decade of its history. I spent more hours than I care to remember in the archives of the Northampton Shoe Museum and sorting through box after box in Dr. Martens own Northampton archive. I travelled to Seeshaupt, near the southern German city of Munich, to meet Dr Funck himself [with Dr Maertens, one of the co-originators of the boot]

and to root out original pairs of
the air-cushioned sole – one of
which was found under the bed
of Funck's son, Matthias. In a
shed in his garden was an
incredible collection of Funck's
'other' inventions, including –
most memorably of all – a
tandem scooter, which simply
comprised a pair of Vespas
welded together.

Throughout the research, the
Griggs family, as well as the
Maertens and the Funcks, have
always been one hundred per
cent cooperative and
enthusiastic. Max and Stephen
Griggs were particularly helpful;
the latter was even at pains to
encourage me to delve into the
more seedy and difficult periods
in the boot's history, so that the
story was told comprehensively
and objectively. I hope that I
have achieved this, but it
remains for you, the reader,
to decide.

So I hope you relish this
strange and fascinating tale.
I doubt that many other stories
I recount will be as diverse,
riveting and truly unique.
Hopefully, you will agree.

Martin Roach
March 2003

Like many great inventions before it, the genesis of the Dr. Martens boot was a strange and peculiar combination of innovative thinking, some insightful commercial sense and a large slice of good fortune. Key to the making of the legend was a rich industrial heritage, although there was little in these early days to hint at the boot's subsequent iconic status.

The Early Years

FOR COMFORT
AirWair
WITH Bouncing SOLES
The ORIGINAL
Air Cushion Sole
Dr. Martens

The Early Years

Long before Dr. Martens became an icon of British fashion, the black boot enjoyed many years as the humble, working-man's footwear of choice. So how did this unassuming boot make that transition from a workwear essential – at one point advertised as a gardening shoe – to one of the definitive cultural icons of our modern times? It is a strange story . . .

The bizarre tale begins in the village of Wollaston, in the county of Northamptonshire, in the British Midlands. The county was the shoe-making capital of the country, and had been for centuries. In the middle of the seventeenth century, during the English Civil War, Oliver Cromwell had marched into Wellingborough to demand no fewer than 20,000 pairs of boots for his Ironside soldiers, thereby laying the foundation stone for the future shoe trade in Northamptonshire. The county's hard-working cobblers were soon drinking in taverns called The Boot Inn or Cedric Arms, the latter named after the patron saint of shoemakers.

Fast-forward to 1901: Queen Victoria died on 22 January of that year; the first long-distance radio transmission was made in morse by John Ambrose Fleming; Giuseppe Verdi, the giant of nineteenth-century Italian opera, died of a stroke; and the Commonwealth was officially named. Back in the sleepy streets of Wollaston, the seeds of a modern icon were being sown. Dr. Martens boots would become a global phenomenon that would be inextricably linked to such cultural ephemera as punk, goth and grunge – a whole wave of modern subcultures and lifestyles that, at the staid turn of the century, would have

seemed (if such things could be imagined) to be from another planet. All this was still many decades away, however, when Benjamin Griggs and Septimus Jones decided to form their boot-making partnership, drawing on their county's long and respectable tradition of fine, handcrafted footwear.

The partnership worked well for ten years, until Jones departed in 1911. At this point, Benjamin and his son, Reginald, formed R. Griggs and Co., with considerable financial support

Right: (clockwise from left)
Dr Maertens measures up; Maertens and Funck; Dr Maertens; Bill Griggs, whose idea it was to contact the pair.

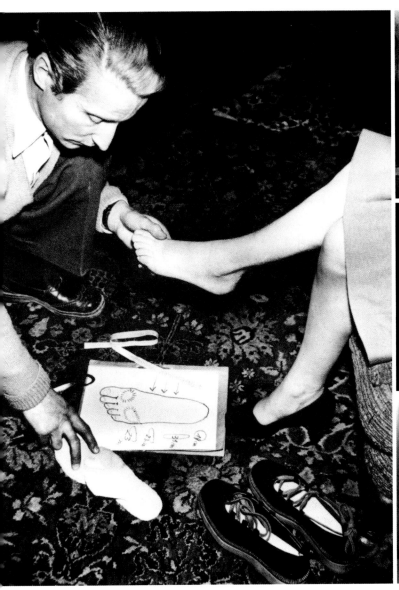

You don't ride on solid tyres why walk on them!

DM1

wear Dr Martens
AIR CUSHION SOLE FOOTWEAR

Air Wair
WITH Bouncing SOLES

FOR MEN·WOMEN·AND CHILDREN

"A soldier in shoes is only a soldier, but in boots he becomes a warrior."

General George 'Old Blood and Guts' Patton

and encouragement from Reginald's grandmother, Jane Griggs. The two-man firm got underway, making all their shoes by hand – within 70 years, their descendants would be manufacturing no fewer than a million pairs a month.

For now, however, the Griggs family settled down to earning a solid reputation for producing hard-wearing, solidly built workwear – mainly heavy-screwed and stitched miners' and army boots. In the light of the boot's subsequent association with skinheads, it is interesting to note that at this early stage one of the firm's best-selling models was the Bulldog Boot. Huge quantities of this boot were bought by the army and marched their way through two World Wars.

The simple yet limited production methods remained largely unchanged until the late '50s. However, by then there

were a dozen or more other notable footwear manufacturers in Northampton, and competition was becoming fierce. Despite this, the Griggs' business managed to remain very buoyant, thanks in no small part to substantial sales to UK National Servicemen and US soldiers in the Korean War.

However, one new boot in particular had arrived that presented a serious threat to the Griggs' future: this was the so-called TUF working-man's boot, manufactured by G.B.Britons. The TUF boot boasted a vulcanized rubber sole and a swift production method that allowed for a vastly higher output than did any of the traditional methods.

By the '50s, three Griggs men – brothers William, Ray and Colin – ran the firm. William, or 'Bill' as he was called, quickly recognized the potentially ominous problems that such a popular competitor as the TUF boot could create for their own firm, and thus started scouring the shoe trade for a solution. Bill formed a co-operative with other ↓

Left: A '60s advert heralds the arrival of the air-cushioned sole. Overleaf: A later advert makes much of the skiing accident that was the catalyst for its invention.

Also in April 1960

- South Africa and indeed the world at large were still reeling from the Sharpeville Massacre, when national police fired on unarmed African demonstrators. Over 178 people were injured and 69 were killed. The excessive use of force quickly became a powerful symbol of the apartheid regime's prejudice and brutality.

- Brasilia, a new city in Brazil, was unveiled. Wrenching the status of capital from Rio de Janeiro, Brasilia was designed in the shape of an aeroplane, with residential blocks as the wings and the government buildings as the fuselage. Within a few short years, the idealistic new city had been ravaged by class divisions, poverty and overpopulation.

- 'My Old Man's A Dustman' by Lonnie Donegan was the best-selling UK single; its US equivalent was the 'Theme From A Summer Place' by Percy Faith.

- The South Pacific soundtrack was at No. 1 in the UK album charts at the start of April 1960.

Dr. Klaus
Maertens.
Inventor,
painter, M.D.
and, fortunately
for all of us,
a damned lousy
skier.

It's said that Dr. Klaus Maertens could do a lot of things.

He graduated from medical school in Munich on July 6th, 1942. He was a passionate, caring physician. He was an incredibly accomplished painter. Legend has it he could even open a bottle of beer using only his back right molars. (Of course, this was back in the days before twist-off caps. When men were men and dentists worked frequently.)

He was what's known as a renaissance man.

But, luckily for all of us, there was one thing he just couldn't do: Ski.

On a frosty morning in 1942 Klaus donned his trusty wooden skis and hit the Alpine slopes. And hit them he did. Hard.

So hard that he injured his foot quite badly.

(Those who were there say it was a spectacular wipeout worthy of the opening credits of ABC's *Wide World of Sports*.)

Klaus quite literally limped home to his drawing board, where he and another friend, a mechanical engineer, Dr. Ing. Herbert Funck, set about inventing a shoe that would offer him respite from his injury. A shoe that would offer him comfort from his ordeal.

Using a soft rubber, the two doctors appropriated from discarded World War II airplane tires, they began to fashion the soles for their new shoes. They worked diligently for days and nights before one of them suddenly had a simple, yet brilliant idea: Put thousands of air bubbles in the soles of the shoes.

Thus in a moment of utter genius was born the Dr. Martens patented, air-cushioned sole. (Some where along the line the "e" was dropped.)

Forty-eight years later, we're still putting air bubbles very much like the originals, in every single pair of Dr. Martens. Of course, instead of abandoned airplane tires, we employ a rugged, yet pliable elastomeric material that flexes when you walk, but will resist oils, alkalies, acids and cooling for many years to come.

The next breakthrough in the world of footwear was a unique patented procedure called "Funck's Process" whereby the AirWair sole is actually heat sealed to the all leather Goodyear welted upper of the shoe.

This allows the Dr. Martens sole and upper to act as one very comfortable, flexible, yet incredibly durable piece.

With all of this innovation in the footwear world coming from one shoe, it's no wonder Dr. Martens became so popular with people who spend long days on their feet. Factory workers, the English police force, and now even English lawyers and accountants.

They have all found Dr. Martens to be an extremely reliable, comfortable and now, though not at first, oddly fashionable shoe.

Now, you may ask, whatever became of Dr. Klaus Maertens? Well, as a matter of fact, he kept on treating his patients and inventing things until the end of his days. But even today, a half a century later, we never forget the man who brought these shoes to the world.

A man, by the way, who couldn't ski if his life depended on it. To find the Dr. Martens outlet nearest you, just pick up the phone today and give us a ring at 800.866.985.

"Mr Ray Griggs said that there is no end to the types of footwear that can be produced. Great interest was being shown, business taken so far was substantial and prospects appeared to be bright . . . the shoes were most comfortable to wear and gave the impression of walking on air."

Extract from *Shoe & Leather News*, 16 June 1960

local firms so as to buy new machinery and speed up production; but even then he kept looking for further advances. In the light of the family's history of supplying boots with which to fight Hitler's Nazis, the slice of genius that inspired the Dr. Martens boot came from an unlikely source – postwar Munich, in Bavaria, southern Germany.

In 1943, Dr Klaus Maertens, a 25-year-old soldier, had been on leave from the Front and on a skiing trip in the Bavarian Alps. He had broken his foot while on the slopes and so returned to his native town of Seeshaupt, near

Munich, to convalesce. While recovering, his inventive mind began ruminating on the possibility of a pair of shoes that would be sufficiently comfortable to relieve his piercing foot pain. He wanted to create a sole made of some type of air-filled material, rather than the conventional – and much harder – solid leather.

Looking back on this several decades later, Dr Maertens explained, 'The week war ended, everyone rushed out and started looting. But while most people were looking for valuable stuff like jewels and furs, I picked out a cobbler's last, some leather,

needles and threads, and made myself a pair of shoes with the thick air-cushioned soles I'd been thinking about.'

With his – albeit rather crudely – handmade prototype boots on his feet, Maertens made his way into Munich to generate interest in his invention. By chance, he bumped into an old university friend, Dr Herbert Funck. Funck hailed originally from neighbouring Luxembourg, but had been raised in Germany. The two had met while studying at Munich University – indeed, for a while they had both vied for the attentions of the same girl.

Funck immediately became fascinated with the peculiar shoes on his friend's feet. After the two men had been talking for a while, Funck, a mechanical engineer by trade, suggested they go into partnership together, fabricating the sole. Funck had kept hold of his Luxembourg passport, so the existing ban on German citizens trading with the American military did not apply. In no time at all, he bought up tons of rubber at rock-bottom prices from the now-abandoned

Right: (clockwise from top left)
Dr Maertens chooses a fashionable fabric for uppers; the team in 1949 displaying their thousandth shoe; an early shoe mould.

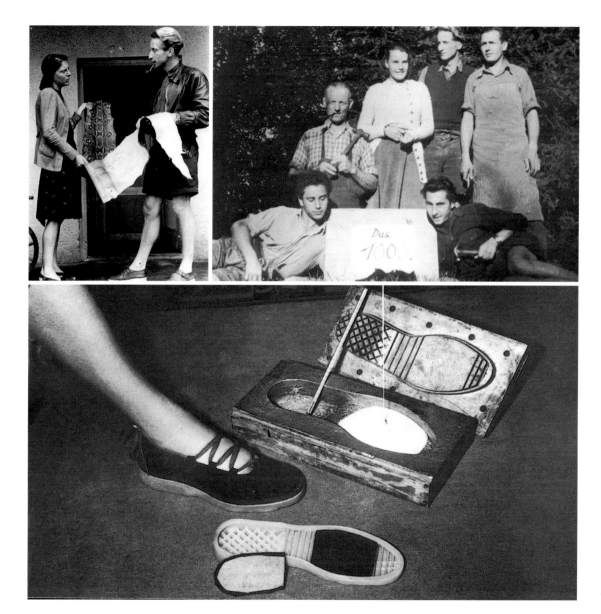

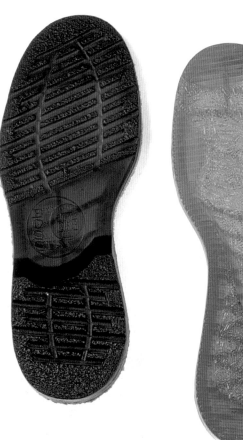

"I'm happy new life's been injected into the boot, but I don't really keep up any more – I'm more interested in my oils, my cars and my country patients."

Dr Maertens, speaking in 1988

Luftwaffe airfields, and began converting them into shoe soles.

Speaking in 1985, Maertens reflected on their combined fortunes: 'Our timing was perfect. The whole of Europe had just spent five years in army boots and everyone knew how uncomfortable they were. The shoe was the right answer at the right time.'

The two friends used various bits of old army uniforms to construct their first shoes. Recalled Maertens, 'I pulled the regimental numbers off my jacket epaulettes and used them as eyelets, and I bought uniform trousers from ex-officers for their leather leggings. I could get two pairs of shoes out of one pair of trousers. But the secret was all in the soles . . .' Whereas the soles of traditional shoes were stitched directly onto the

upper of the shoe, Maertens invented a process whereby the two were heat-sealed together, thereby forming a series of strong, air-cushioned compartments.

In 1947 the two men started handmade shoe production in Seeshaupt. The early versions of the shoe were a cross between a brothel creeper (a crepe-soled shoe) and a boot. At this stage, they bore no resemblance whatsoever to the fabled Dr. Martens boot; only the sole hinted at the iconic boot yet to be invented.

For now, this new type of footwear proved exceptionally popular in Germany, especially among older women, who appreciated its comfort and durability. Indeed, such was the shoe's popularity that Drs Maertens and Funck were forced to open a factory in Munich in 1952. Right through the '50s, 80 per cent of the sales of their

Left: An early German prototype sole, flanked by two later English versions.

Also in 1960

- *Record Retailer* (later to become *Music Week*) publishes the first UK album chart.

- Senator John F. Kennedy becomes President of the United States.

- Heart pacemakers are first implanted.

- Felt-tip pens are launched.

- Drinks in aluminium cans are sold for the first time.

- Nuclear aircraft carriers take to the waves.

- Weather satellites are first used by meteorologists.

- The decision by publishers Penguin in London to publish D.H. Lawrence's *Lady Chatterley's Lover* after a controversial court case marked a new era in freedom of speech.

- Alfred Hitchcock's *Psycho* is screened.

- The VW Beetle, originally conceived in 1920 but not manufactured in Germany until 1945, starts to sell in the US.

"Don't let your vanity be imposed upon by those persuasive articles on wearing pin-point heels for shopping in the morning . . . The number of males on the loose during shopping hours is narrowly limited."

Extract from *The Intelligent Woman's Guide to Good Taste*, 1958

shoes came from women over the age of 40. During the same decade, the range expanded to include over 200 different styles of shoe. By 1959, they were advertising their invention in overseas' trade magazines.

While scanning the pages of *Shoe & Leather News*, the British shoe-trade magazine, Bill Griggs' eye was caught by Maertens' advertisement for potential licensees of his revolutionary new sole. Bill lost no time in contacting the pair, and so it was that Griggs acquired the exclusive license to produce the air-cushioned sole.

A few key changes were made before the boot was launched. For example, the elongated German heel was altered to assume a more rotund and orthodox shape for the British shoe-buying public. As the intention first and foremost was to market the boot as workwear, a strong leather upper with a pronounced bulbous shape was attached, together with a distinctive yellow welt stitch. Griggs further developed the shoe in the direction of the now-famous silhouette by designing a two-toned and grooved sole edge and a unique sole pattern.

The new brand name that the Griggs family bestowed on this latest shoe to come out of their workshop was AirWair, after the air-cushioned sole. Its unique identity was further reinforced with a black-and-yellow heel loop, featuring the word AirWair and the slogan 'With Bouncing Soles'. The script used was based on Bill Griggs' own handwriting, and taken directly from the doodles that he had drawn while coming up with the brand name.

Legend has it that the original boot was intended to have an oily finish so as to be suitable for wear by porters and other workers in the fish markets of the East End of London. However, a rogue batch slipped through uncoated and proved to be equally durable while more appealing to the eye.

The Griggs brothers toyed with both 'Dr Funck' and 'Dr Maertens' as the name for the new brand. The two of them opted for the latter, however, worried that the former would sound too much like Dr F*ck. The choice of name was then anglicized, simply by removing the first 'e', which had given the pronunciation '*mare*-tins'.

Hence on 1 April 1960, the very first Dr. Martens boot rolled off the production line at the Griggs' factory. Taking its name from the date of its inception, the classic eight-hole, cherry-red 1460 had arrived.

Right: (clockwise from top left) Dr Maertens holds one of his ladies' shoes, prized for their great comfort; two early styles; the AirWair logo on a Dr. Martens shoe box. Overleaf: Workers from a Desborough shoe company, later to be part of Griggs, on a day out in 1914.

Made in ENGLAND

STYLE

DESCRIPTION

B1461

SIZE	BLACK GIBSON SHOE				FITTING
6	CONSTRUCTION Dr. MARTENS WELTED	SOLE & HEEL PVC	LINING MAN MADE	UPPER LEATHER	

JUNE . 2

1914.

A humble advertisement in a shoe-trade magazine launched the legend – over the course of the next ten years, the Dr. Martens boot would become the subject of a seemingly insatiable demand, as youth culture snatched the 1460 from the safety of its workwear origins and cast it headfirst into the seething world of subcultures.

60s

'60s

As the very first pair of Dr. Martens 1460 boots rolled off the production line in Northampton, England, the world had just entered a new decade. It would turn out to be one of the most eventful decades of the twentieth century.

The decade was also to provide a somewhat incongruous backdrop for the infancy of such a functional boot. Perhaps symbolic of the huge changes and seismic shifts that would take place was the 'space race'.

What had started in the late '50s with Russian space missiles weighing in at just a couple of hundred pounds, and continued with Yuri Gagarin's voyage as the first man in space in 1961, would end with a man walking on the surface of the moon.

It was to be a decade of rebellion; one that would witness revulsion at a controversial South-East Asian war and a swelling tide of deep dissatisfaction with the establishment among the younger generation. Radicalism was about to reach into almost every corner of modern life. Women's rights, civil rights, the anti-war movement – change was afoot. Elsewhere, polio was

virtually eradicated. Yet, as an antidote to faith in medicine, when polled most Americans who smoked still said that the habit had 'a beneficial effect'. The launch of the contraceptive pill (actually the result of a laboratory contamination) was also set to transform women's lives, quite literally overnight.

Early research into harnessing nuclear power for domestic fuel consumption suggested that free, unlimited energy for the whole population might not be an impossibility. However, the more sinister role this recent development could take was brought sharply into focus by the Cuban Missile Crisis of 1962, with the threat of mass thermonuclear Armageddon.

Kennedy opened the decade for the Americans by defeating Nixon in the US presidential election. The dashing JFK was a Second World War hero, a people's favourite with a

beautiful wife. He became the youngest-ever president of the US and perhaps the world's first truly telegenic leader. The relationship between politics and television would never be the same again. Likewise, throughout the '60s, television progressed from being a rare – and luxurious – novelty to a staple of everyday life.

The Bay of Pigs invasion, the failure of the US to achieve a rapid defeat of the Viet Cong in the Vietnam War, and the hardening of lines in the Cold War between the nuclear superpowers, made the '60s an uncomfortable and, at times, terrifying era in which to live. This was nowhere more apparent than in the seismic impact of the assassination of

**Right: (clockwise from top left)
Gagarin on his historic space flight; Jimi
Hendrix; domestic appliances transform
the home; 'Swinging London'.**

"Serious Injury Avoided.
Mr Joseph Baker of Newcastle-on-Tyne has good reason to be thankful for having worn boots made by Messrs. R. Griggs and Co. A stone of about 6ft by 3ft fell on his shoulder and foot. Whilst his shoulder required profuse stitching, his foot only suffered a blackened toenail."

Extract from *Shoe & Leather News*

John F. Kennedy in November 1963, which shook America to its very foundations and, overnight, fuelled the formulation of the modern 'conspiracy theory'.

Rock 'n' roll

Britain, by contrast, had 'never had it so good'. So said popular prime minister Harold Macmillan, and for much of the '60s few could argue with him. Consumerism in the modern sense took hold, with all sorts of household gadgets, such as electric stoves, vacuum cleaners and refrigerators, being made

Left: Boot tag.

available for the first time. The postwar boom almost made 'housewifery' a fashion once more, if the cheery, anodyne and at times outrageously chauvinistic television adverts were to be believed. Thus consumer spending was buoyant, technology offered increasingly ingenious 'mod cons' for the home, and employment and the economy were robust. Furthermore, Britain was about to enter an explosively fertile period in its cultural history – the so-called 'Swinging Sixties'.

The '50s had seen the birth of the 'teenager'. For previous generations, the years between childhood and adulthood were merely a transitional phase during which youngsters aped what their parents wore, thought and did, in a rather benign apprenticeship for their own maturity. However, postwar affluence spearheaded by Macmillan's Conservative government quickly began to alter this status quo for good.

The economy was so strong that national labour shortages were more of a problem than snaking unemployment queues. Consequently, young workers (often as young as fifteen) were being taken on in ever-increasing numbers and, due to the shortages of staff, were able to expect healthy wages. With their wallets bursting with disposable income, these teenagers scoured the high street for something on which to spend their money before – or after – they had to enrol for eighteen months' military National Service, and they found it in rock and roll. For the money men behind the new musical phenomenon, teenagers were the perfect consumers.

Rock and roll had begun to blend the music of black culture, R&B and boogie with new – and often white – performers, and its appeal was undeniable. It had

"It's a fact! The working man has never before been offered a really comfortable boot. Hard work – hard boots had to be accepted. The revolutionary Dr. Martens Air Cushioned soles puts an end to this foot-breaking torture . . . a most pleasant experience for the much abused foot."

1960s advert for Dr. Martens

arrived in the late '50s in a blur of hip-swivelling and hair curls and, despite premature predictions of its downfall and unfavourable comparisons with late '50s fads such as trad jazz and skiffle, rock and roll in 1960 was well placed to capture the imagination of millions of teenagers around the world. Elvis, Cliff Richard and Bill Haley were at the forefront, but behind them was a legion of talented rock and rollers.

The '50s had introduced the first true teenage subculture – teddy boys. Citing early American rockers as their source, teds openly courted society's disapproval. Fashion-wise, they were as much in debt to the Edwardians as to the rock and rollers. Teds played on the stylistic themes of the upper-class dress of the 1900s, the Edwardian era in England (hence their name, abbreviated from 'Edward'). They dressed in tight 'drainpipe' trousers, unusually long jackets with trimmed collars and cuffs (called Drape coats, because of their cut), colourful waistcoats, string ties, pointed boots (called winkle-pickers) or crepe-soled suede shoes (called brothel creepers), the whole topped by elaborate quiffs. Female teds looked more

to American styles of clothing, wearing full, calf-length circular skirts with 'beehive' or long ponytail hairstyles. Teds were pilloried in the conservative press for rioting at cinemas, as Britain tasted its first blast of public teenage hysteria. In short, the '60s was the first full decade to have the recently evolved 'teenager' unleashed upon it.

The deaths in February 1959 of Buddy Holly, Ritchie Valens and Big Bopper in a plane crash near Clear Lake, Iowa, USA, are often cited as the end of the first phase of rock and roll. Indeed, the music scene of the '60s soon became recognizable as a very different beast from that which had held sway during the previous ten years. 'Beatlemania' was the most tangible example of this sea change. At the same time, this phenomenon was also the start – and, arguably, the crowning moment – of the global export of British youth culture.

After The Beatles had conquered Britain in 1962 and 1963, their UK chart success quickly translated into global domination, with America falling under their intoxicating spell. Incredibly, a group of four mop-topped Liverpudlians who had ↓

Right: Beatlemania.

Original construction of a boot

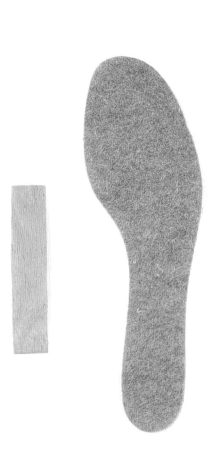

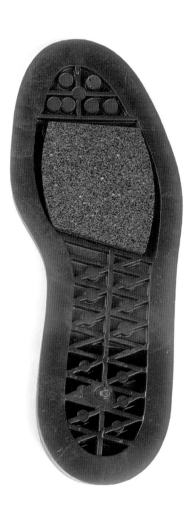

Early prototype

These gleaming but unassuming workwear boots are in fact one of the original pairs of German boots to have been manufactured in large quantities by Dr Klaus Maertens and Dr Herbert Funck. The boots are now carefully preserved in the archives at Dr. Martens.

"Since the introduction of the miniskirt, rape is up 68 per cent in the US and 90 per cent in England."

The police adopt a "softly-softly" approach to growing crimes against women.

entered the decade as virtual unknowns, finally were 'bigger than Elvis'.

England, and in particular London, had replaced Paris as the fashion capital of the world, with names such as Mary Quant being bandied about by the young and style-conscious. The designer had revolutionized women's wear with the then scandalous miniskirt. She also introduced the familiar geometric prints and incorporated them into soon-to-be ultra-fashionable clothes that sold by the million. The Mini motorcar – best seen in the movie *The Italian Job* – and the first generation of supermodels, spearheaded by the waif-like Twiggy, also reinforced the notion that British was best.

Twiggy was a 16-year-old Cockney girl whose real name was Leslie Hornby; her ultra-thin figure soon earned her the nickname that made her famous. Her popularity was certainly not confined to the UK

– when she travelled to the US, she was treated like a conquering pop star by screaming fans. At the time, her tiny frame, clad in knitted tops and miniskirts, represented the very opposite of haute couture and reinforced the growing awareness of the power of youth. This atmosphere of youth and creativity infected culture around the globe to the extent that other innovators, including Andy Warhol, Bob Dylan and the head of Motown, Berry Gordy, also enjoyed huge success.

The impact Beatlemania in particular had on the popularization of British culture is incalculable. Musically, it was responsible for the first major invasion by British acts of the hitherto predominantly indigenous US charts. With this sonic saturation smothering the globe, fashion and style inevitably followed, or rather went hand in hand. The media quickly focussed on the garish colours of Carnaby Street, and

international magazines such as *Time* raved about the merits of 'Swinging London', with its bohemian shops and idiosyncratic designers, photographers, models and entrepreneurs. Nearby Newburgh Street, in Soho, actually hosted many of the most popular shops, too, and the King's Road in Fulham was equally influential, as the world looked to Britain for a fashion lead. Everyone aspired to the neat suits, distinctive haircuts and lifestyle of the Fab Four.

During the first half of the '60s, the infant Dr. Martens boot seemed a highly unlikely fashion item. This was a dazzling time for footwear, with the vibrant culture being reflected in the use of bright colours on string-thin sandals, wild styles such as exaggerated platforms and even materials previously the preserve of science fiction films (vinyl, plastic) being used by shoe designers inspired by the accelerating space race.

A whole range of different styles of footwear had also recently emerged, including loafers, sandals and chisel toes. At the same time, boots were involved in fashion like never ↓

Right: DM's become the preferred work shoe due to their hard-wearing soles.

SOLES
RESISTANT TO

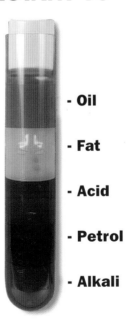

- Oil
- Fat
- Acid
- Petrol
- Alkali

Kinky Boots

Dr. Martens have found themselves involved in some of the more extreme lifestyles since their inception in the '60s – but none closer to the fringes of society than the fetish scene.

The boot's black, bold look – particularly when made of patent leather – has proved hugely popular within some of these fetish circles. It has also enjoyed its share of wearers who are even more particular in their tastes. They are the foot fetishists.

Some trace this peculiar penchant back to Chinese footbinding (which, incidentally, first affected men, not women). Foot fetishism, or podophilia as it is scientifically termed, is widely accepted as having originated in some largely forgotten childhood experience.

The most obvious modern roots can be traced back to this decade when, in the 'Swinging Sixties' in London, PVC and leather clothes enjoyed something of a heyday. The experimental fashions of the day allowed designers to produce some quite risqué outfits (for the time, at least), the popularity of which was sufficiently notable to filter into the mainstream. So it was that celebrities such as Honor Blackman (as Pussy Galore in *Goldfinger*) and Diana Rigg (in *The Avengers*) could be seen sporting such materials on television.

Ted Polhemus, in his book *Street Style*, credits a designer called John Sutcliffe with these early statements of fetish fashion. Sutcliffe was a man who continued to create such gear even after the fickle tides of mainstream fashion had moved on to other styles. He made particular mileage out of designing for private clients, an indication of the underground scene that refused to disappear, and a fact also reflected in the existence of magazines such as *Pussy Cat*.

At that time – and despite the liberality of '60s London – fetishism was still something of a taboo subject. Over the years, however, this stigma has mostly dissipated. The punk years revitalized an interest in fetish fashions in general, and in many senses sent the style truly mainstream. The most tangible example of this was Malcolm McLaren and designer Vivienne Westwood's provocatively named SEX shop in London.

Foot fetishism is now so widely acknowledged that it contains various groupings, which include bare feet, dirty feet, feet in stilettos, trampling, crushing, tickling and even the comically named 'footjobs'.

With regard to Dr. Martens – and other boots – the fetish is usually allied with some form of submission or dominance. Often the boot wearer will be female and the powerful image of the eight-hole will be the prime attraction for the fetishist.

"The Chinese have probably had the longest romance with feet, going to extreme measures in creating erotic effects."

Extract from the book, *The Encyclopedia of Unusual Sex Practices*

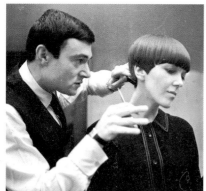

"This is the face of '66 – Twiggy, the Cockney kid with the face to launch a thousand shops and she is only 16."

The *Daily Express* announces the world's first supermodel

Also in 1961

- Valium is introduced.

- East German authorities close the border between East and West Berlin and begin erecting the Berlin Wall.

- The US announces a minimum wage of $1.15 an hour.

- Alan Shepard makes the first US manned space flight on 5 May.

- American writer Ernest Hemingway and Hollywood film star Gary Cooper pass away.

Also in 1962

- The Beatles, a mop-topped foursome from Liverpool, release their first single, 'Love Me Do'. The record only reaches No. 17 in the UK charts.

- Over 90 per cent of US households now have one television.

- Diet-Rite becomes the first sugar-free soft drink.

- The first James Bond movie, *Dr. No*, starring Sean Connery, opens.

before – the stylish Chelsea boot, the Cuban-heeled Beatle boot of Fab-Four fame, the Clarks desert boot and the knee-high so-called 'kinky boot' were all very popular. Even the ladies' ankle boot, based on a style from the 1800s, had made something of a comeback. Nancy Sinatra even sang about go-go boots in 'These Boots Were Made For Walking'.

Fortunately for Griggs & Co., the rather clumpy Doc Marten boot had an entirely different sales base – as a workwear item, its original and chief purpose. Sales of DM's were almost exclusively provided by postmen, policemen, medics, factory workers, builders, London Underground staff and other blue-collar workers. With a price tag of just £2 at their launch, the first boots were soon joined by the plain three-eyelet

Derby shoe, known as the 1461 (after the date of its inception, 1 April 1961). This proved particularly popular with the General Post Office, which has been one of the main buyers of the shoe over the years.

Although the boot was popular with policemen, it was not until the late '70s that Dr. Martens became standard uniform (some forces stipulated that the trademark yellow welt stitching had to be coloured in with black ink to meet strict regulations). The soles, which were resistant to oil, fat, acid, petrol and alkali, proved particularly useful for dealing with leaking car fuel at the scene of traffic accidents. Some officers claimed the soft soles proved invaluable when sneaking up behind criminals, while others maintained that the high-legged quarters offered extra protection against attack.

Possibly the first public figure to be seen wearing Dr. Martens was Member of Parliament Tony Benn. Born Anthony Wedgewood Benn, this socialist MP was ↓

Left: (clockwise from top left) Vidal Sassoon creates a short crop; men are prone to vagaries of fashion; shoes are over the top; clothes whimsical.

The 1460

On 1 April 1960, the eight-eyelet 1.4.60 was born. There was no fanfare to herald the boot's arrival, or hint of its subsequent iconic status. Built for work, the Dr. Martens quickly became a favourite among England's working classes. Its famous yellow stitching, two-tone grooved sole and signature footprint made it a classic.

> "It was a laugh. I haven't enjoyed myself so much in a long time. It was great – the beach was like a battlefield."

An 18-year-old mod talks to British tabloids about the famous coastal clashes

actually a Viscount – Viscount Stangate – but, turning his back on his privileged roots, he championed workers' rights and other related issues. He was often seen marching at the front of crowds of CND (Campaign for Nuclear Disarmament) protestors in his button-down cloth shirts and grey suits, complete with black 1461 shoes.

It was a style that was copied in later years by figures from across the political spectrum – 'Trotskyist' lecturers and *Socialist Worker* students often wore Docs as a sign of political affiliation with the workers for whom they campaigned, who trudged to their jobs each day in boots just like theirs.

Meanwhile, as yet unaware of the merits of the 1460, British youth culture continued to mutate and evolve. Although 'Swinging London' had made

Left: Skinhead culture now manifested itself in many corners of British life.

England the focus of the mainstream fashion world, there was a vibrant and complex cauldron of youth subcultures bubbling under, too, perhaps best exemplified by the mods-versus-rockers battles of this highly charged period.

Booted for battle

Mods and rockers rode their scooters and bikes to Britain's coastal towns to do pitched battle on the golden sands. Especially popular were national holidays, or Bank Holidays.

The media was there to capture the fighting in all its black-and-white glory, as no picturesque resort seemed safe from the hordes. Dr. Martens found no place on the feet of these modern-day vagabonds. Yet it was through the inevitable fragmentation of the mod subculture that the boot was first seized upon and dragged into the seething, seedy underbelly of British youth.

Also in 1963

- President John F. Kennedy is assassinated.

- Cassette recorders and lung transplants first introduced.

- Martin Luther King makes his famous 'I have a dream...' speech at the Lincoln Memorial, in front of 200,000 people.

- 'Sex began in 1963.' So said poet Philip Larkin.

- The Great Train Robbery in England nets nearly $7 million in cash for the thieves.

Also in 1964

- South Africa extends the powers of its apartheid regime, sending eight prominent black leaders – including a young Nelson Mandela – to jail for shockingly lengthy prison sentences.

- The Warren Commission Report issues its findings on the J.F.K. assassination, which are that Lee Harvey Oswald acted alone – however, this conclusion is greeted with widespread scepticism.

> "In the national horror league, skinheads weigh in somewhere between serial killers and devil dogs. It's as if shaving your head and lacing up a pair of DM's turns you into some sort of dangerous alien life form."

George Marshall from *Spirit of '69 – A Skinhead Bible*

When the violent mods-versus-rockers battles died down after their peak in 1963–4 (at least in the eyes of the bored media), splinter groups emerged within the mod ranks. From them sprang a culture that was, paradoxically, to prove the making of the Dr. Martens boot and also, in later years, the brand's potential unmaking: skinheads. The more flamboyant types grouped together to form the trendy mod scene, while a sartorially more minimalist section evolved into what became known as 'hard mods'. Proud of their working-class roots and repulsed by the evolving, effeminate and liberally minded 'Summer of Love', hard mods espoused the everyday workwear of the proletariat.

Often based in grim postwar council estates in areas such as Bethnal Green in the East End of London, these groups are seen by many as the precursor to the skinhead movement, and were seen sporting crops, jeans and 'big boots' as early as 1964.

These early skinheads listened to soul and Jamaican ska, with parties in Brixton and Lambeth introducing them to new music as well as to the highly influential Kingston rude boy scene that had migrated from the Caribbean with young Jamaican immigrants. Also around at this time was the terrace bootboy, and it was the combination of these three disparate cultures that ultimately merged to form the skinhead movement.

One of the first instances of skinheads appearing recognizably in public came during the Great Vietnam Solidarity March in London in 1968, when 30,000 anti-war students were heckled by 200 or so closely cropped local youths dressed in Millwall Football Club's team colours.

Although skinheads had indeed been around in some form or another as early as 1964, the term was not actually coined until near the end of the decade. Other early names included cropheads, lemons, no-heads, baldheads, prickles, spy kids and boiled eggs.

Most inappropriate of all, perhaps, was peanuts – said to have arisen because the engines of skinheads' scooters (stripped-down, practical versions of their mod forefathers' extravagant machines) made a sound like a peanut rattling around in a tin. 'Bovver Boys' is taken from the slang euphemism of 'bother', as skins would often go out 'looking for bother'.

Contrary to popular belief, the British skinhead style is not actually a descendant of the American crew cut, which leaves no hair at the back and sides,

Right: Button badges were a way for skins to declare their allegiance.

> "The sight of cropped heads and the sound of heavy boots is cause for sinking feelings in the pit of the stomach."

Chris Welch, *Melody Maker*, 1969

and a longer top crop. Despite this fact, American military leaders were so scared that their English-based servicemen would be mistaken for skinheads while off duty that they issued a memo allowing them to wear hairpieces. Others have claimed that the skinhead cut originated among dockers, who shaved their heads as a preventive measure against hair lice.

Most skinheads chose haircuts between number four on the barber's razor and number one, the shortest. Since this allowed little room for self-expression, permutations on the hairline were popular – either square cut, rounded or following the natural line. West Indians sometimes shaved a pencil-thin parting in the cut (they called their crop a 'skiffle'), and this habit caught on with UK skins.

Left: Standard-issue 1891 DM's twelve-holed boots.

Later, other skins sported a so-called 'dark shadow', where the razor was used without a guard. Baldness was not popular. The occasional large sideburns, known as 'mutton chops', were cherished.

Skinhead girls opted for a feather cut, which was cropped short on top of the head with delicate wisps over the ears, face and neck. This was often accompanied by fishnet stockings, monkey boots rather than DM's, and short skirts.

Interestingly, at this early stage the haircut was considered less important than the heavy boots, which were the defining item of clothing. In the initial stages, Docs were hardly worn at all; instead, monkey boots, National Coal Board miners' boots or army boots were popular, usually with no more than eight or nine holes. It was not until skinheads adopted the Dr. Martens boot that its place in modern subculture was assured. ↓

Also in 1965

- Sony introduces the first Betamax home video recorder.

- US aeroplanes bomb North Vietnam in the first deployment of troops in that territory.

- Over 500,000 communists, leftists and ethnic Chinese are massacred by the military in Indonesia in an attempt to topple the increasingly unpopular independence hero, President Sukarno.

- Militant black leader Malcolm X is assassinated.

- Singer Nat King Cole passes away.

Also in 1966

- England wins the football World Cup against West Germany at Wembley Stadium, sending a jubilant country into ecstatic carnival celebrations.

- *Luna 9* lands on the moon, paving the way for man's first steps on the moon by Neil Armstrong three years later.

- *Star Trek* debuts on TV, and ushers in the most famous split infinitive in television history – 'to boldly go'.

British and brash

These boots, although manufactured much more recently, hark back to the heady days of the 'Swinging Sixties'. Incorporating the Union Jack flag into their design, they proudly advertise their national identity and playfully evoke the theme of 'British is best'.

By a strange quirk of fate, Dr. Martens didn't become popular until their steel-toecapped predecessors (which, in a few instances, had spikes welded onto them, although not by Griggs) were classed as 'offensive weapons' by the football police and confiscated outright when spotted. This quickly led to Docs becoming almost standard issue for the skinhead, with some skins wearing them several sizes too big in order to exaggerate their presence. The boots had that appealing uniformity of look for the average skinhead, who craved such gang-like adherence. Also, their simple utilitarian design was both an anti-fashion statement and a nod of recognition to their working-class roots.

The simple fact of their being very comfortable also sold them to the skinheads, plus the fact that they polished up better than any rival boot. This is one element of skinheads that is often overlooked – their attention to detail in their appearance, a characteristic they inherited from the mods. As they needed no time to style their hair, skins spent literally hours on their clothes and footwear, polishing their DM's almost obsessively. One peculiar trend was to 'antique' the boots. This involved polishing a pair of cherry-reds with black shoe polish, which was then rubbed off, leaving rivulets of black in the creases.

Skins also used a repair technique called 'hot-knifing', whereby the heated blade was inserted into the split sole and pressed back onto the upper – a tip actually described in Dr. Martens early in-box literature. (The technique has also been used for unlawful purposes, although never involving Griggs, with some illegal exports of Docs containing drugs stashed in the cavities of the sole, which is split open, filled with the illicit goods and then sealed with a hot-knife. Even some official export shipments of Dr. Martens have been stopped at Customs to check for this.)

This cherishing and extensive polishing is indicative of the fact that for many people, not just skins, DM's are worn in rather than wearing out, and each pair is regarded with great sentimental affection. Put simply, the boots gain more character and improve with age.

The rest of the skinhead look was uncompromisingly working class, reactionary even. When set against the flamboyant 'Flower Power' culture and high fashion of the '60s, it was a real counter-culture statement. Trousers were worn short so as to display the boots, whose long laces would often be tied through the famous AirWair heel tag. American-style button-down shirts manufactured by brands such as Jaytex, Brutus and, of course, Ben Sherman, were the favoured look, always worn with the top button undone (and at this stage plain; checks didn't appear until the early '70s).

Red-tag button-fly Levi's were the other most popular accoutrements for the skinhead, though sometimes corduroys were also worn. The best-looking jeans were old and faded; but as the denim material was so strong, a bottle of bleach was often thrown over them to speed up the ageing effect. These Levi's were supposed to be worn around the hips, but skins wore them higher around the waist, thereby requiring braces, which varied in width and colour.

Skins in different countries resorted to different colour codes for laces and braces (although none seemed universal). Thus white laces might signify allegiance to the ↓

Right: Simaryp produced the ska anthem 'Skinhead Moonstomp'.
Overleaf: Early DM's advertising.

AirWair
WITH Bouncing SOLES
Genuine, Original and Unique
Dr. Martens
WITH THE WELTED AIR CUSHION SOLE

National Front in the United Kingdom, while in Canada yellow was purported to designate a police killer.

The skin with a little more money could afford an Abercrombie coat, known as a 'Crombie', which was often worn with a handkerchief folded and tie-pinned inside the breast pocket (despite rumours to the contrary, there is no definite colour code for these handkerchiefs). This could be for smart wear, as could a tonik suit made from mohair or in Prince of Wales checks, most often with twin or single vents and narrow lapels. Even the buttons on the sleeve were a measure of style, usually numbering three or four. Brogues or loafers often replaced treasured Docs for such smart outings.

Musically, the early skins were into reggae, soul and ska. They championed artists such as Desmond Dekker, Max Romeo and The Pyramids. Many a youth club was filled with black kids and white kids dancing to the same songs, mingling freely without a hint of trouble – a fact that makes a mockery of the later racist elements within the skinhead movement. Unfortunately, however,

Left: Skinheads wearing Crombies.

increasing levels of violence began to turn public opinion against the skinheads.

In the spotlight

It wasn't long before the skinheads' very distinct style began filtering into the media and cultural ephemera of the day. In late 1969 The Pyramids recorded their famous 'Skinhead Moonstomp' under the pseudonym of Symarip. The title was a direct reference to the supreme comfort of the Dr. Martens air-cushioned sole, which fans described as being 'like walking on the moon'. The B-side, 'Skinhead Jamboree', hails the skinhead uniform in its lyrics, mentioning both Doc Martens and Levi's.

The first book on the subject is widely regarded as having been *Skinhead* by James Moffat, writing under the pseudonym Richard Allen. In the novel, which has sold several million copies, Moffat created the most famous skinhead of all time – Joe Hawkins, racist, sexist and violent. Moffat, a native of Canada, wrote over 400 pulp-fiction novels before he died of cancer in 1993.

The skinhead phenomenon even infected parliament where, in 1969, the Labour Prime Minister Harold Wilson berated

Also in 1967

• First heart transplant performed in Cape Town, South Africa.

• Che Guevara is captured and killed by Bolivian Ranger Troops; meanwhile the Arab–Israeli Six Day War rages in the Middle East.

• *Rolling Stone* magazine is launched in San Francisco.

Also in 1968

• First Philadelphia Bank installs the first automated cash dispenser.

• Waterbeds and Jacuzzis are invented.

• Martin Luther King is shot dead by a sniper in Memphis – widespread rioting follows.

• *Planet of the Apes* and The Beatles' *Yellow Submarine* are showing at cinemas.

• *The Electric Kool-Aid Acid Test* by Tom Wolfe is published.

> "They talk quite happily about the way guitarist Pete Townshend smashes his guitar against an amplifier when the mood takes him. Pete says it produces an unusual sound and I can well believe him."

Alan Smith in *NME*, June 1965

certain Tory rivals as 'the skinheads of Surbiton'.

Like all subcultures, that of the skinhead soon started to evolve and fragment. One descendant was the suedehead, a look that began to appear around 1970. Suedeheads were skins who grew their hair slightly longer, probably to avoid the stigma of being dubbed a skinhead. Their name originated in their hairstyle, which they preened with steel combs.

Suedeheads wore tonik suits and Crombie coats during the day and sometimes even carried umbrellas and the occasional bowler hat (umbrella tips were often filed to a sharp point and then re-painted black). Their footwear tended to be patterned brogues, known as Royals, rather than Docs. The boots were too hard, too military in appearance and hence largely shunned, as indeed they were by the next skinhead hybrid, the short-lived smoothies.

By 1972, the first wave of skinhead was effectively over. The violence, the anti-social image and changing fashions had robbed the movement of much of its potency. However, the look had embedded itself deep in the psyche of British youth. During the late '70s, the second wave of skinheads prowled the streets with, in many cases, a much more sinister right-wing edge to them. That time could be described as possibly Dr. Martens darkest hour, with tabloid newspapers screaming headlines and showing pictures – seemingly daily – of Dr. Martens-clad skins. In one extreme instance, an elderly lady was pictured on the front of a tabloid with a livid, black bruise across her face in the shape of a Dr. Martens air-cushioned sole.

For many brands, this image alone would have signalled their death knell. Fortunately, Dr. Martens infection of so many other subcultures meant that by the end of the '70s it was no longer the preserve of the skinhead. There were even signs that skins themselves were starting to look elsewhere, particularly when the black 1460 became an increasingly common item of police uniform.

This second wave exported the look successfully to all corners of the globe. Thus Australia became home to one of the biggest skinhead populations outside of the UK, after the British mass migration to that continent during the '60s. Germany acquired a large following, too, although right-wing extremists there adopted the look, doing little to popularize the image within the mainstream of that country.

It can be argued that the less savoury elements of the skinhead movement placed Dr. Martens in a perilous dilemma at times. On the one hand, the aforementioned images of ↓

Right: High Wycombe skinheads.

Pinball Wizard

The Who's links with Dr. Martens went past Townshend's own preferences. Their superb 1969 rock-opera double album, *Tommy*, was described by one critic as 'the most important and innovative rock album since *Sgt Pepper*'.

In 1975 director Ken Russell turned that magnum opus into a film in which, during the performance of the classic 'Pinball Wizard', Elton John narrates the story of the deaf, dumb and blind kid while perched on top of an enormous pair of brown Dr. Martens. The boots were made of fibreglass and stood 54 inches tall – Elton's size-four feet were fitted into another pair of shoes, which were strapped onto the towering twelve-holers. (Afterward, Elton kept the boots.) In 1988, at a London auction of rock 'n' roll memorabilia, the current Chairman of AirWair, Stephen Griggs, bought the boots for £12,100 (the event was sparked by Elton wanting to clear out some rooms to redecorate; it raised over £4 million). The over-sized DM's now stand proudly in a glass showcase at Northampton's Shoe Museum.

The Who's contribution to film didn't stop at *Tommy*. Their much-anticipated 1973 double concept album, *Quadrophenia*, became a cult classic when the big-screen movie version was released six years later. It is seen by many as one of the best British films ever made. The setting was 1964, the peak of the mod–rocker battles. The story tells the tale of the young mod, Jimmy – played by Phil Daniels – struggling to assert himself amid a destructive cocktail of girls, drugs, violence and growing up.

Jimmy's complex yet endearing character was said to be made up of all four of The Who's personalities – the meaning of the word 'quadrophenia'. He rides around on his beloved scooter, talks about – and tries to sleep with – girls, and takes copious amounts of uppers and downers, ending up in jail for his troubles. Jimmy wrote himself into mod legend when finally he cracked and drove his scooter over a cliff.

Interestingly, The Who deliberately excluded themselves from the film in order to reduce its appeal to mainstream America. Instead,

Right: Elton John as the Pinball Wizard's nemesis.

Above: Mods in *Quadrophenia* clothing.
Right: The Who.

a relatively unknown cast was chosen. Even Sting, who had two lines as the moody but cool Ace Face, was only just coming to prominence as lead singer of The Police. *Quadrophenia*'s broad Cockney accents and highly stylized clothes, plus the soundtrack, the association with The Who and the brilliant script, made the film a classic almost overnight. 'Jimmy the Mod' doesn't actually wear Docs in the film, nor do they appear on anyone else's feet – but the

scooter and mod revival provoked by the movie's release saw the boots being worn by an entirely new generation (see chapter on the '80s).

This 'modernist' movement had started off as a secretive working-class cult in the clubs and cafés of Soho, west London, in the late '50s, surfacing publicly in around 1962. The original mod look was nothing if not cosmopolitan, with Italian suits, French haircuts and British shirts. Historically, they had blood ties with America's Cool School Jazz men and Italy's so-called pavoneggiarsi, but it

was the British mod who crystallised the trend. The Who themselves enjoyed a considerable mod following, despite the fact that their own mod incarnation as The High Numbers and their later single, 'I'm The Face', proved a flop.

Phil Daniels later became a Royal Shakespeare actor, even appearing in an RSC performance of *A Clockwork Orange*. He also formed a band of his own, called Phil Daniels and the Cross, who released one eponymous album, and he went on to make a cameo appearance on Blur's hit single 'Parklife',

Joe Casely-Hayford

"Based on the idea that Dr. Martens transcends the superficiality of fashion, I made my boots inside out to highlight the consistent quality of this product and the importance of inner integrity."

"It is almost a fantasy land of sights and sounds. Flute-players in robes, micro-minied girls in boots, without bras . . . swing down the streets."

US writer Professor Lewis Yablonsky

battered pensioners and street violence was the stuff of PR nightmares. Yet on the other, the skinhead subculture was responsible for single-handedly wrenching the boot away from the workplace, and giving it instant popularity and currency in the underbelly of Britain's youth culture.

With that transformation came a massive increase in sales. Current President Max Griggs explains: 'Suddenly, the skinheads adopted them. Demand rocketed almost overnight. Instead of 1,000 pairs a week, we were being asked for 6,000 pairs and we needed a system to cope with that. Over the next few years, we had to introduce an allocation system, whereby customers were scheduled in for so many pairs only. We were always able to undersupply the market and keep it hungry. The more I told

Left: The classic cherry-red 1460 boots.

people they couldn't have any more, the more they wanted.' When combined with the integrity of the boot's working-class roots, its durability and apparent openness to change, the 1460 was already on its way to becoming an icon of style.

By the late 1960s, the growing popularity of 'Flower Power' had erupted in the so-called 'Summer of Love', and the mood of the times made the mods-versus-rockers fights seem like a dim and distant memory. American influences had returned to infect youth culture in the UK.

The Haight-Ashbury scene in San Francisco was one geographical hub of 'Flower Power', and LSD was the drug at its core. With the trend toward greater communal awareness came a sea change in fashion – kaftan coats, coloured sunglasses and all manner of extravagant ethnic hippie clothes became the order of the day.

- Apollo 11 lands astronauts Neil Armstrong and Buzz Aldrin on the moon, on 21 July, prompting – from Armstrong – the now often (mis)quoted statement: 'That's one small step for a man, one giant leap for mankind.'

- The rubella vaccine is unveiled; as is the jumbo jet.

- The Stonewall Riots in New York are widely seen as heralding the birth of the modern Gay and Lesbian Rights movement.

- Concorde makes its first fare-paying supersonic flight across the Atlantic.

- Children's programme *Sesame Street* debuts on cable television in America.

- A year for famous deaths, including those of 'Beat' generation writer Jack Kerouac, actress Judy Garland, actor Boris Karloff and boxer Rocky Marciano.

- John Lennon is quoted in the *Daily Express* as saying, 'I'm down to my last £50,000.'

- US troops in Vietnam number 550,000; their peak in the country.

> # "History's largest happening . . . one of the significant political and social events of the age."

Time magazine on Woodstock

This counter-culture movement dominated much of the late '60s and, although it was initially driven by a socio-political thirst for change, it eventually became so consumed by mainstream culture that it represented little more than a fashionable whim. By contrast, skinheads detested hippies and the two subcultures could not have been farther apart in their look, lifestyle and beliefs.

Trouble and strife

Flower Power was at heart a pacifist movement. But by 1968 certain sections of society were no longer happy to make peaceful protest alone. Growing groups of dissenters, concentrated mainly at colleges and university campuses around the globe, began to foment and then execute increasingly militant protests.

The European mainland had opened the decade with the erection of the Berlin Wall; this was to remain a symbol of political separatism and social polarization for the following three decades.

Only a few years after the Wall went up, Europe was ravaged by demonstrations, as disenchanted Baby Boomers demanded radical change. Varying levels of violence met them, from outright slaughter of left-wing demonstrators by police in Mexico to almost commonplace brutality by authorities elsewhere. The loose-knit movement was christened the New Left and saw communists demonstrate alongside anarchists. It was sufficiently destabilizing as to lead to the fall from power of both Belgian and Italian premiers. Charles de Gaulle's republic was 'brought to its knees' by the student demonstrations of May 1968.

Britain in the late '60s was experiencing problems too, with the devaluation of the pound and more difficult economic troubles looming on the horizon for then Labour prime minister Harold Wilson. Young people across the globe were starting to take an interest in matters other than what they were wearing and who they were listening to. Just as music and art had become deeply experimental, so then did the political and social thinking of this younger generation. Suddenly, it dawned on them that they could change the world. A new era of protest was being born.

Fortunately, the rather fey and lightweight music of much of Flower Power was countered by a growing interest in heavier guitar rock – perhaps best exemplified by the breathtaking brilliance of The Who. Pete Townshend of The Who was one of the first high-profile figures to wear Dr. Martens. Against a backdrop of flowery, effeminate styles, Townshend's choice of Docs was a beacon of austerity. Thanks to The Who's volatile live show and Townshend's characteristic guitar jumps and kicks, the boots were captured in scores of pictures. Townshend even wrote about the boots in his song 'Uniforms'.

Despite their latter-day status as stadium rock gods, The Who's place in modern subculture is secure. Initially, however, many

Right: Hippies on the corner of Haight and Ashbury, San Francisco.

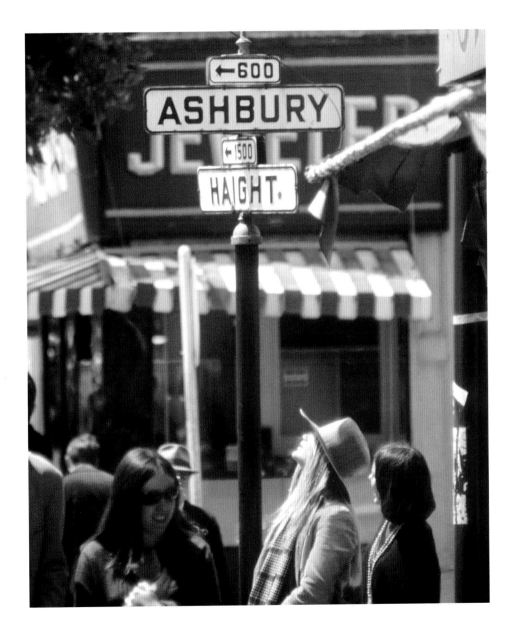

"Rock is very, very important and very, very ridiculous."

Pete Townshend, 1994

people failed to recognize their potential. When Decca was handed the original master tape of the seminal 'My Generation' single, the record company refused to accept it, complaining that the feedback at the end of the track was unplanned distortion. This was only moderately less embarrassing than EMI, which turned The Who down altogether.

Once signed to the rather more visionary Brunswick label, The Who's 'My Generation' single quickly saw the band, and songwriter Townshend in particular, being hailed as spokesmen for the disaffected youth of the day. The song's stuttering, speed-fuelled lyrics and brilliant instrumentation (including one of the greatest bass solos of all time, courtesy of John Entwistle) secured The Who a place in rock history on both sides of the Atlantic.

This was just one of dozens of classic Who tracks, described by Townshend himself as 'sweet

Left: Pete Townshend, mid-flight, during one of his trademark leaps.

songs sung by a violent group'. Townshend was brimming with such enlightening one-liners, which include what is alleged to be the briefest rock interview of all time – to *Rolling Stone* magazine's Cameron Crowe, Pete announced, 'I've changed my mind.'

The Who's live show attracted much attention, not just for the spectacle but also for its aggressiveness, which horrified the establishment. The band's genius drummer, Keith Moon, often had to tie his drum kit together with rope because he hit the skins so hard. Considered by many to be the greatest rock drummer of all time, 'Moon the Loon', as he was nicknamed, was a whirlwind of energy at the back of the stage.

While John Entwistle provided the solitary calm exception in front of him, Daltrey and Townshend were frenetic. The guitarist's windmilling arms bashed away at his bruised strings, often climaxing in the guitar neck being punched through the speakers or simply smashed into pieces on the floor.

When Townshend first met Roger Daltrey, he told him he had 'been buggering about on guitar for years getting nowhere'. This was typical of the many brilliant, unpredictable and frequently acerbic quips that Townshend fed to the media over the years, which helped to fuel his reputation as one of rock's most articulate, inspired and inspiring forefathers.

The end of the '60s saw man walking on the moon – a fitting culmination of a decade of tremendous change in the world. In music, the following years, 1970 and 1971, saw the deaths of three leading of rock's lights – Jimi Hendrix, Janis Joplin and Jim Morrison – as, tragically, the personal consequences of much of the previous years' drug culture began to become apparent.

For Dr. Martens, although the company's sales were still predominantly within the workwear sector, a pivotal and crucial breakthrough had been made. The skinhead culture that would, at times, seem an impossible burden, had changed the course of the brand's history forever. For the shoemakers back in sleepy Northamptonshire, nothing would ever be quite the same again.

Komodo

"We have taken something that is quintessentially
British and added something typically Balinese . . ."

This was the decade that cemented Dr. Martens place in youth culture. It was a period when mad haircuts ruled the world, when the flames of the tribes of youth were at their most distinct and yet shone most brilliantly. Despite this clear gulf between each youth subculture, the Dr. Martens boot was already showing its unique capacity for longevity and adaptability.

70s

'70s

The hazy psychedelia and free-loving ideals of the late '60s quickly faded at the turn of the '70s.

The new decade was heralded by a turbulent sequence of sharp reality checks: the dismal failure of the Vietnam War, Nixon's humiliation and the subsequent exposure of a deeply embedded climate of political corruption, plus the arrival of militant feminism, proactive civil rights and – last, but not least – widespread economic disarray.

The OPEC (Organization of Petroleum-Exporting Countries) oil problems of 1973, during which the price of crude rocketed by 200 per cent – plunging the world into an energy crisis – served mostly to highlight the fact that the impending fossil-fuel shortage was approaching with ever-more worrying velocity. Sitting in long lines for petrol, this was the first time many people had paused to consider just how vital such energy was to their lives (they were to be reminded of it with another shortage, in 1977).

Many saw the plethora of global issues and problems now besetting the '70s as a hangover from the explosion of ideas, cultural evolution and social development that had characterised the '60s. Whatever the cause, the repercussions of such potentially cataclysmic events filtered quickly down to the man on the street, and Britain was not immune from the feverish instability of the global economy.

The Conservative prime minister at the time, Edward Heath, son of a carpenter and builder, had taken Britain into the European Common Market in 1971, thereby fanning hopes of a new dawn of Continental unity and domestic serenity. However, between 1970 and 1974, steep rises in the prices of commodities and oil forced Heath to adopt stringent policies to combat inflation. Heath's term in office was also coloured by the deployment of troops in Northern Ireland.

More damaging, perhaps, the UK's miners and other workers went on strike, and three-day working weeks became commonplace. Heath's subsequent defeat in the General Election of 1974 was seen by many as a result of his opposition to the striking miners. Interestingly, his replacement as Tory leader – a certain female Member of Parliament by the name of Margaret Thatcher – was seen initially as a no-hope 'stalking-horse' candidate.

As the '60s turned into the '70s, there were already signs of festering social unrest. In keeping with Dr. Martens rather unsavoury early history, the menace of football hooliganism soon found a place for the 1460. Opinions differ as to precisely when this violent phenomenon started, but the general consensus is that the 1968–9 season provided a watershed, with aggressive skinhead mobs prowling the terraces.

Right: (clockwise from top left) '70s fashion; a punk rocker; women's lib takes to the streets; refuse collectors fail to collect during a wave of strikes.

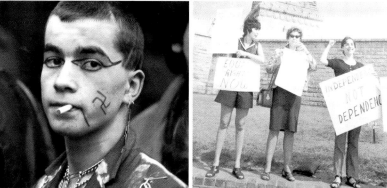

> "You have to forget about what other people say, when you're supposed to die, or when you're supposed to be loving. You have to forget about all these things. You have to go on and be crazy. Craziness is like Heaven."

Jimi Hendrix

In the wake of England's 1966 World Cup triumph, attendances at soccer matches had reached record levels – a buoyant employment market had created a swathe of affluent youth able to afford to travel to matches away from home. With this increasingly 'territorial' activity, which coincided with a renewed patriotism courtesy of the government's 'I'm Backing Britain' campaign, violence was on the increase. The football 'firm' was born.

Despite their hostile intentions, there were nonetheless still interesting stylistic characteristics to these groups – they were, in short, the epitome of terrace fashion.

Left: Police force football fans to surrender their DM's in the hope that this would prevent match violence.

Some wore white butchers' coats with team names displayed across the back; the so-called 'Chelsea Headhunters' firm even splattered their white coats with blood for that extra bit of authenticity. Later on, others dressed as droogs from the cult movie *A Clockwork Orange* (see feature, p.96).

The early '70s saw the first pairs of painted Docs on the football terraces. Team colours were most common, although white was also popular. Steel toecaps were frequently exposed for extra menace and were the preferred weapon of abuse. Police forces across the country rapidly declared such boots to be 'an offensive weapon'. In response, toecaps without the steel became popular, which provided an unlikely sales boost for Dr. Martens.

Even without the steel toecaps, DM's could still wreak substantial damage, forcing the police to devise a new tactic. They insisted that anyone wearing Docs remove their laces, the theory being that far less harm could be done with a loose boot; terrace charges were thus rendered well-nigh impossible. The fans quickly counteracted this by smuggling in spare sets of laces in their trousers. Police spotted this and banned shops in the locality from selling laces on match days – in response, the hooligans would thread paper clips or wire into their jacket linings.

Sometimes, girlfriends were enlisted to smuggle items into stadiums, as women were less likely to be searched. With no other option left to them, the police introduced the ultimate deterrent – forcing fans to take their boots off altogether. Policemen then stood guard over these bare-footed hordes until the opposition fans had left for home. After that, a massive free-for-all would ensue, as people tried to reclaim their own boots, and sometimes a newer pair belonging to someone else.

It wasn't just the Dr. Martens boot that was used in conflagrations. A veritable arsenal of weaponry found its

> ## "When she [mum] came in the next morning to wake me up, all she could see was this great big pair of Dr. Martens at the end of my bed and my bald head!"

Noddy Holder, Slade

way onto the terraces – bottles, blades, darts, razors in oranges, throwing stars, lead piping and even a 'Millwall brick' (a newspaper rolled up so tightly that it formed a thick, hard club). Small coins and paper were often improvised with to form impromptu knuckle-dusters.

When police started separating opposition fans inside the ground, the violence only spread outside to railway stations, trains, cafes, pubs, anywhere in fact. Indeed, one of the most famous firms of all, West Ham's ICF, travelled exclusively on Inter City trains, hence their name (short for 'Inter City Firm'). Other notorious firms included Portsmouth's 6.57 Crew (named after the time of the train they would catch on match days to avoid the police), the Chelsea Headhunters and the Millwall Bushwackers.

It is perhaps curious that the '70s are often tagged – unjustly – as a decade of novelty fads and joke fashions. True, these ten compressed years brought us Little Jimmy Osmond, pointed collars and flared trousers, Chopper bicycles, *The Brady Bunch*, Big Macs with fries, *Dallas* ('Who Shot JR?') and *Kramer vs Kramer*.

However, this was also an era that saw the birth of the modern feminist movement, equal-pay campaigns and racial equality laws, the founding of the Open University (bringing higher education to the working masses), the Sex Discrimination Act, the first test-tube baby, the microprocessor, the barcode, early incarnations of e-mail, Space Invaders, the emergence of rap and hip-hop, Apple and Microsoft and the word 'internet'. It was a time of truly seismic upheavals.

Likewise, Dr. Martens entered the '70s in a very different position from how it would exit those years. In 1970, it was a workwear item, a boot for the masses, but one largely devoid of subcultural poignancy. Yet when the haze of glitter, 'bondage' trousers and *Saturday Night Fever* had passed, the humble 1460 closed the decade firmly established as one of the great British style icons.

This transition was mirrored in the explosion of youth culture witnessed during those years. Although the start of the decade was overshadowed by the deaths of Jimi Hendrix, Janis Joplin and Jim Morrison (rock's 'leading lights'), some inspiring and at times revolutionary music would emerge from this bleak beginning – and DM's played a large part in this evolving scene.

Glam rock

The transformation from workwear essential to cultural staple started inauspiciously enough with DM's playing a very minor role in the glam rock movement. With The Beatles having split up only a year ↓

Right: (clockwise from top left)
Marc Bolan of T-Rex; David Bowie as
Ziggy Stardust; Slade sporting full 'glam'
regalia; Iggy Pop.

Warren Noronha

"Dr. Martens have an inherent punk rock image and my inspiration came from wanting to soften and inject them with a little elegance and sexiness. At first glance the boots look a little like an old piece of Victorian furniture and then as you look closer you see that the pictures are quite pornographic. First perceptions are not always true."

"About four years ago I gave a pair of Martens to a mate of mine, the Skunk. He's dead now. He said to me, 'Are these the originals on the front of *New Boots and Panties!!*?' I said, 'No.' But he wanted a letter of authentication to auction them at Christies. I gave him the letter, but he didn't quite pull it off."

Ian Dury

Doc Trivia

- Current President of AirWair, Max Griggs' passion for football has seen him involved in Rushden & Diamonds soccer team, as well as Dr. Martens sponsoring West Ham United.

- Ian Dury once called Dr. Martens 'a communistic shoe' because of its mass-produced nature mixed with its ability to allow individuality. The boot can indeed be both a badge of conformity and a symbol of personal uniqueness.

previously, a new music arrived that instantly made the Fab Four and even the '60s themselves seem like eons ago. English charts were popularized by novelty hits, squeaky pop or the denim-clad, so-called 'blues boom'. Then, from the glitter-spangled ether came the first real glam artist – Marc Bolan.

Although his band, T Rex, had charted with their debut single in 1968, Bolan's genius shone brightest in the early '70s, with hits such as 'Jeepster', 'Telegram Sam' and 'Metal

Guru'. David Bowie followed and captured the glam crown with Ziggy Stardust and the Spiders from Mars, while the less critically revered but nonetheless commercially huge likes of Slade, Sweet and the now-disgraced Gary Glitter swelled glam's ranks.

Glam – or glitter rock, as it is known in the US – is the butt of many knowing critics' jokes in the new millennium. It even seems possible that the outrageous look of artists such as Slade's Dave Hill will never – whatever cycles recur – become fashionable again. Yet glam was not entirely superficial. Glam

Left: Dave Hill in suitably understated costume.

"Revolt is understandably unpopular."

Alex Trocchi, from *Invisible Insurrection of a Million Minds*

gave us Ziggy, and it led us deviantly toward albums by original rebels such as Iggy Pop and Lou Reed. It was at once light-hearted and yet subversive. Glam, like punk after it, was all about shocking.

Most strikingly perhaps, glam challenged traditional gender roles. It encouraged kids who watched *Top of the Pops* to dress extravagantly, to wear make-up, to fantasize about Bowie, whether they were boy or girl. Radios across Britain filtered odd, Stardust-soaked, asexual vocals into factories, cars, offices and shops across this staid and – on the surface at least – sexually conservative island. Androgyny became the peak of fashion and thousands of teenagers fell under glam's spell, in the process spewing out a new generation of latter-day stars, such as Echo and the Bunnymen's Ian McCulloch, Suede's Brett Andersen and Placebo's Brian Molko.

McCulloch's own favourite record of all time reveals much about the impact of glam on his peer group: 'Ziggy Stardust is head and shoulders above any other. It made me want to be a singer in a great band and have a great hairdo. I wanted to be Bowie or Ziggy. At thirteen, Bowie looked like the best thing I had ever seen. I didn't fancy him; he just looked so good. It hit me at exactly the right age and I was a sucker for all of it, completely innocent. Over that six-month period I felt things that I have never come close to since. Being a father and a husband are the best feelings. Yet nothing buckled me under quite like Ziggy Stardust. I was on another planet for six months. For a while there I *was* Ziggy Stardust.' (Notably, when McCulloch's own band, the Bunnymen, were at the height of their fame in the early '80s, many of their raincoat-wearing fans religiously wore DM's.)

Of course, at the heart of glam fashion was the platform boot. Iggy wore a colossal silver pair; Gary Glitter's were towering; Bowie and his legendary guitarist Mick Ronson did the same. Even more mainstream artists – and certainly thousands of impressionable high-street customers – wore platform boots en masse. Eight-inch heels covered in sequins, glitter and multi-colours were commonplace. TV series such as *Wonderwoman* proved highly popular and fuelled the interest in extravagant boots, which were usually worn with hot pants.

Knee-high platform boots were frequently covered in glitter, and sometimes painted with flowers – a precursor to the later fashion for customizing DM's in the '80s and '90s. The platform is one of the few essentials of the glam look that has enjoyed several subsequent reincarnations as popular fashion items over the years.

Dr. Martens utilitarian design essentially meant that the boot could only observe the glam rock revolution from afar. (Fans of Slade, however, distanced themselves from other glam band followers by proudly sporting DM's rather than orthodox platforms.) At times, it seemed that the monochrome simplicity of the Dr. Martens 1460 could not have been further from the fashion of the day. At this point, 90 per cent of Docs were still the eight-hole classics, with three-eyelet shoes filling the rest of the market. Cherry red and black were the only two colours available.

Right: Glam-rock fashion saw some bizarre trends in footwear.

"You should try everything once except incest and Morris dancing."

Sir Arnold Bax, classical composer

As a result, DM's struggled against the lurid spectacle that was glam rock. Those few glam kids who did customize their Docs often used bicycle spray paint, as this had all-important metallic glitter in it. In the world of pure pop, DM's occasionally managed to hold their own against the tidal wave of glam – fans of teeny-bop sensations the Bay City Rollers wore eight-hole Docs along with their tartan scarves, which dangled from their teenage wrists.

Yet some championed the boot for the very reason that it was the polar opposite of the trend, and could thus be seen as a clarion call to simpler times. Likewise, sandals and pumps also found new popularity among the disenfranchised minority. Other more academically minded critics had loftier theories about the negative effects of the platform. In his book, *The Sex Life of the Foot and Shoe*, William Rossi argues that the '70s platform boot caused a decline in the

birth rate, because it was so asexual as to extinguish any desire between the sexes.

Seeking out the origins of some glam bands, however, reveals that DM's could, after all, boast some genealogical significance, necessarily via the cornerstone of DM's' early youth appeal: the skinhead. The first true British skinhead band was Slade, who went on to develop a glam rock image and reap the benefits with scores of hits, including 'Mama Weer Al Crazee Now' and 'Cum On Feel The Noize'. The Wolverhampton band enjoyed six No. 1 hits and even made their own feature film, *Slade In Flame*. This, together with numerous TV appearances, showcased two of music's most unlikely pop heroes – the heavily sideburned Noddy Holder and horizontally fringed Dave Hill.

However, back in 1969, when skinheads were first starting to come to public prominence, a long-haired Slade were playing a four-month residency in the Bahamas as a reggae and soul backing band. Yet, as the cover of their debut album, *Play It* ↓

Left: The original skinhead band, Slade.

Also in 1970

- A new type of data: barcodes.

- Mini-Moog synthesizers are introduced.

- Canadian film-makers invent giant projector IMAX system.

- The world's population reaches 3.63 billion.

- The Beatles split up, having released their last album, *Let It Be.*

Also in 1971

- The microprocessor is introduced – a computer on a chip, its inventors promise that it will revolutionize the world. Most people are doubtful.

- The cellphone is invented.

- Led Zeppelin release their masterpiece, 'Stairway To Heaven'.

- It costs the average US taxpayer $125 to fund the Vietnam War – yet only $7 of the same taxpayer's money goes to medical research.

- Britain goes decimal with its currency, amid widespread media warnings of impending economic and social chaos.

Paul Smith

"Dr. Martens are normally associated with strength, toughness and workwear. Our design was a complete contrast to this . . . meant to add a sense of fun."

A Clockwork Orange – A Vicious Strangeness

The violent fractured edges of society – and Dr. Martens involvement in it – did not stop at the football terraces. On 20 December 1971, Stanley Kubrick's controversial, Oscar-nominated film premiered to both underground acclaim and mainstream outrage.

Based on the Anthony Burgess book of the same name, the film centres on the scientific 'rehabilitation' of Alex Delarge (played by Malcolm McDowell), a brutal gang leader whose violent life leads to a prison sentence from which he is released on condition that he undergo a 'cure for criminals'. This involves mind-altering drugs, which create nausea and illness if the subject should think of sex, violence, or even so much as contemplate the mildest form of anti-social behaviour.

This invasion of Alex's civil liberties, set against the backdrop of his gang's own dark, depraved activities, created a compelling paradox. The inclusion of the film's own vocabulary – the gang members were called 'droogs', the language itself named 'nadsat' (seemingly half-Cockney; half-Russian) – only added to its allure, as did the affront caused by the 'ultra-violence', namely graphic acts of barbarity, including sexual assaults. This hard edge, the brutal subtext and the highly stylized art direction gave *A Clockwork Orange* all the trappings of a cult classic.

Kubrick was given the Burgess novel as a present by Terry Southern, who had co-written the acclaimed *Dr Strangelove* screenplay with him. Kubrick is reported to have read the lengthy novel in one sitting, then immediately turned back to page one and started again. The central character of Alex instantly appealed to him, later leading Kubrick to compare him to Richard III: 'Alex, like Richard, is a character whom you should dislike and fear, and yet you find yourself drawn very quickly into his world and find yourself seeing things through his eyes.' He claimed to have hit upon the choice of McDowell for the part after only a few chapters.

The cinematography of the film was a cornerstone of its huge critical success, and a hint at Kubrick's earlier career as a professional photographer (he had also had a stint as a

Right: Original poster artwork by airbrush artist Philip Castle.

STANLEY KUBRICK'S
CLOCKWORK ORANGE

professional chess player to fund his early film-making efforts). Only four sets were built for the film. Instead, Kubrick featured gritty, inner-city tower blocks, filmed at Thamesmead, in south-east London, west London drugstores and Oxfordshire family homes.

The atmosphere this created, when spliced with Burgess' enthralling yet deeply disturbing vision of the future, was a strange dichotomy of ultra-normality and extreme fantasy.

When the film was withdrawn from circulation after a 61-week run, its status as a taboo yet acclaimed masterpiece was assured. Numerous myths exist to explain the ban, but most circulate around the perpetration of copycat acts of violence, which a headline-hungry media instantly labelled 'clockwork crimes'. Judges, police forces and even defendants squirming in the dock – all claimed the consequences of the film were wreaking social havoc.

In one particularly sickening sexual assault, which precisely mimicked a scene from the film, a woman was attacked while her assailants sang 'Singing in the

Left: Skinhead droogs pose outside the Albert Memorial in Kensington.

Rain'. Police were even getting reports of violent youths dressed in exactly the same way as Alex. In the immediate aftermath of the film's withdrawal from circulation, some youths started wearing the distinctive white outfits, black bowler hats and clumpy boots, a hybrid of City-gent style and bootboy intimidation. The banning of the film meant that poor-quality pirate videos quickly started to spring up in the backstreets, thereby only adding to its illicit appeal. Even Kubrick and his family were said to have received death threats, which could well have fuelled his desire to see the film withdrawn.

Ironically, the large black boots that feature so heavily in the film are not actually Dr. Martens. However, in the aftermath of its release, those who chose to follow and mimic the style tended to opt for DM's. As always, a cross-over between musical subcultures existed, with several bands drawing directly on the film. Major Accident, The Violators, Blitz and The Clockwork Soldiers all openly admired Kubrick's work, while California's Durango 95 took their name from the car driven by the droogs. The Adicts were perhaps the biggest fans, with lead singer Monkey

Clockwork Trivia

- Alexander DeLarge is named in a newspaper story late in the film as Alexander Burgess.

- On the release of *2001: A Space Odyssey*, Kubrick counted 241 walk-outs of the cinema by film executives, one of whom was overheard saying, 'Well, that's the end of Stanley Kubrick.' (The film won him his only Oscar.)

- Public outrage at this violence was rabid; some critics argued that the hooligans should be torched with a flame-thrower.

dressing up from head to toe as a 'Clockwork skin', and aping Alex Delarge's disconcerting grin to perfection. Their album artwork also depicted scenes from the film.

New York-born Kubrick enjoyed the rare directorial pairing of commercial success and sweeping critical acclaim. He was never afraid to deal with highly controversial subjects, including underage sex in *Lolita*,

the ultra-violence of *A Clockwork Orange* and the crushing desperation of the harrowing Vietnam classic *Full Metal Jacket*.

Other films in Kubrick's portfolio include *Spartacus*, *2001: A Space Odyssey*, *The Shining* and his last movie, the Tom Cruise–Nicole Kidman vehicle, *Eyes Wide Shut*. On 7 March 1999 – only one week after Kubrick had arranged for a

Above: Tortured genius, Stanley Kubrick. Right: Alex and partners in the movie's vicious rape scene.

special screening of this last film with two Warner Brothers studio executives and the film's two stars – he died in his sleep at his home in Hertfordshire, England. He was 70 years old. *A Clockwork Orange* was finally rereleased in March 2000, nearly twenty years after its initial run.

Caroline Charles

"Dr. Martens are very masculine and remind me of strong women with independent characters . . . I've made them feminine and flirtatious."

"Fuck the fiddly bits."

Joe Strummer's early take on music

Loud, showed, they were about to undergo a dramatic image change that lasted for three full years.

Lead singer Noddy Holder picks up the story: 'We were looking for an image that would set us apart in the clubs and ballrooms. At this stage, skinhead was far more about fashion than any politics. We were working-class lads from the Black Country and so the street look came fairly naturally to us. Adopting that skinhead look gained us overnight recognition – suddenly, everyone knew it was Slade.

'We had no problem getting live gigs in the early days – even the universities who didn't like the skinhead look still booked us because we were a great live band. Most skinheads were into reggae and ska, but we played more soul in a rock vein, even some Motown classics. Skins never adopted us solely as their band, so our audiences were always very mixed. The image worked very well for live shows, but TV and radio didn't give us

much work – the producers were frightened of us.

'So after a while we started to change. We didn't ditch the skinhead look entirely, though – we kept the short trousers but made them far more colourful. We also kept the hair essentially short but grew it very long at the back. At this point, it wasn't called glam rock and there was really only us and Marc Bolan doing this stuff. When we did return to skinhead clubs, they were flabbergasted!'

Slade sported some of glam's most outrageous outfits (and mullets), with Noddy's mirrored top hat being a particular highlight. Underneath the hat, the 'hairstyle' was similarly exaggerated. As Noddy recalls, 'I had my hair cut in London and I was living with my Mum. Our manager, Chas Chandler, took us to get our crops done by the bloke who gave Jimi Hendrix his wild-man look. We bought the Docs from an Army & Navy store and went back to my mother's at 4 a.m. She hadn't seen me for a few days and when she came in the next morning to wake me up, all she could see was this great big pair of Dr. Martens at the

Left: Noddy Holder sporting his mirrored top hat.

Also in 1972

- Sony sells the Betamax home videotape system.

- Nike, the future giant of sports footwear and clothing, debuts.

- Bobby Fisher becomes the first American to win the World Chess Championship.

- Atari releases 'Pong', widely recognized as the first-ever commercial video game.

- Screen versions of *The Exorcist* by William Peter Blattey and *The Day of the Jackal* by Frederick Forsyth premier in cinemas.

- Bloody Sunday in Londonderry, Northern Ireland, sees 13 Catholics killed and 17 injured as British troops open fire on a crowd of peaceful protesters.

- *Apollo 16* lands on the moon.

- Watergate erupts in America.

- The films *The Godfather* and *Cabaret* are both released.

- Eight Arab commandoes infiltrate the Olympic village in Munich, killing two Israeli team members and kidnapping nine others.

"I'm lucky. Somehow by doing what I want to do, I manage to give people what they don't want to hear and they still come back for more. I haven't been able to figure that one out yet . . ."

106

Neil Young, 1979

Dr. Martens – The Story of an Icon

end of my bed and my bald head! She freaked out! My mates called me The Pinkhead or Don the Blue Head.'

Across the Atlantic

'Glitter rock' was never as successful in the charts as its commercially all-conquering glam British cousin. Some cite the first US glam rock band as Zolar-X, who openly aped the *Clockwork Orange* look. In New York, glam and punk often blended into one another (think of the New York Dolls), whereas in the UK the two were polar opposites. In many ways, such differences hinted at the ways in which musical trends in the US and UK would continue to diverge throughout the '70s.

After the demise of The Beatles, the US favoured the heavier rock of Led Zeppelin, as well as other stadium bands such as Crosby, Stills and Nash and The Who, followed by the romantic pragmatism of Bruce Springsteen. The UK, on the other hand, plumped for glam rock and ultimately punk, two-tone and all manner of subcultural splinter groups. Before then, however, there was one musical development of note into which Dr. Martens slotted quite naturally, and this was the so-called 'pub rock' scene.

In America, Springsteen, 'The Boss', was enjoying a burgeoning profile courtesy of his mammoth live sets and working-man, grass-roots imagery. Meanwhile, as much of Britain was about to be caught up in the sneering cynicism of punk, a 35-year-old musician from Upminster, Essex, was writing brilliantly witty, sensitive and musically gifted songs. Enter Ian Dury. One of rock music's great characters, Dury had been struck down by polio at the age of seven. Undimmed by this affliction, Dury's academic and creative talents blossomed, and he was teaching art until the age of 28.

Inspired by his idol Gene Vincent (to whom he later penned a tribute), he turned to music, and in the early '70s started playing the pub circuit in London. Soon after, he formed his band Kilburn and the High Roads, mastering old R&B classics and injecting them with his own brand of incisive and insightful lyrics (usually half-spoken in his inimitable Cockney accent, with rhyming slang). By 1975, Dury was at the heart of the pub rock scene, limping around on the stage sporting his polio stick, cutting an unusual figure as the eternal misfit.

Pub rock shone as a lone beacon of integrity in the mid '70s, when the contemporary scene was awash with bloated mega-groups and corporate, cocaine-snorting rock. On both sides of the Atlantic, prolonged and tiresome prog rock and AOR (Adult Oriented Rock) was ruling ↓

Right: Ian Dury and the Blockheads make pub rock fashionable.

For Design Sake

"This design was inspired by vintage clothing and pop collectables. We used similar reconstruction techniques as in our collections, real gold leaf and enamels to give them a glossy foil-like appearance."

"Punk is a symptom of the way society is declining. It could have a shocking effect on young people."

A British politician and Punk critic, 1977

Also in 1973

- Pink Floyd release *Dark Side of the Moon*; it fails to reach No. 1 in the US but goes on to remain in the Billboard charts for an incredible 625 weeks – over thirteen years after its release.

- French painter, sculptor and giant of twentieth-century art Pablo Picasso dies at his home in Mougins, in the South of France.

- January ceasefire of US troops stationed in Vietnam.

Also in 1974

- Global recession and rampant inflation strike fear into the hearts of economists worldwide.

- India detonates its first atomic bomb, joining the US, USSR, Britain, France and China as a nuclear power.

- *The Joy of Sex* by Alex Comfort is published, prompting outrage in certain quarters.

- The group Abba win the Eurovision Song contest with their performance of 'Waterloo', launching the foursome on an international musical career.

the charts and the airwaves. Even The Who's Tommy was seen by many critics as forming part of this narcissistic scene, and was cited as an example of music having lost its way. Pub rock was the first reaction against such decadence, and it is generally acknowledged as punk's precursor. Other groups who featured in this scene were Brinsley Schwarz, Dr Feelgood and Bees Make Honey. They played R&B covers and back-to-basics blues mixed with some original material, and deliberately chose small venues for their performances, with Islington's Hope & Anchor pub being the key London gig.

Ian Dury's critically acclaimed solo album, *New Boots and Panties!!* (on the cover of which he wears DM's) saw him recognized as one of the country's most original songwriters. The album spent a year in the charts. Dury later went on to enjoy a No. 1 single –

with his band the Blockheads – with 'Hit Me With Your Rhythm Stick', a funky classic that was his only chart-topping success; perhaps somewhat surprising for a man who enjoyed such wide critical acclaim. In the late '80s he turned to acting and even wrote a musical, called *Apples.* His acclaimed 1998 album, *Mr Love Pants,* and his dignified handling of the colorectal cancer that finally killed him in 2001, cemented Dury's remarkable legacy. He is now rightly regarded as one of the UK's most original songwriters of all time.

Away from the music scene, Dury was an unusual bedfellow for the mass of progressives, left-wing students and art-school types who adopted Dr. Martens as their own in the middle of this decade. Sales of the 1460 boot still ruled, but the shoe version was blossoming and seemed to be slowly edging its way into the domain of politics and radical thought, despite its proximity to the

Left: Punk poet Ian Dury.

"Those gobbing little shits would hang around trying to blag in for free with fuck all else but boredom to play with. They would devote hours to personal graffitti, painting anarchy symbols on their Docs, brassing the eyelets with nail varnish remover and letting the world know that nothing is permanent."

Rat Scabies of The Damned

much-maligned skinhead movement.

Indeed, the establishment of the three-eyelet shoe as the left-winger's footwear of choice resulted in a curious 'meeting' of opposites. For, from this point onward, many a Doc-clad skinhead rally would clash with hordes of anti-Nazi campaigners or socialist protesters, separated in the middle by the police; all present would be dressed dramatically differently, except for one thing – their choice of footwear.

The year 1976 was an eventful one. Concorde made its first commercial supersonic flight;

Chinese leader Mao Tse Tung died; Apple Computers was founded by Steven Jobs and Stephen Wozniak; the English dictionary opened its arms to two new words – junk food and sound bite; NASA's Viking I space probe beamed back the first-ever pictures of the surface of the planet Mars; and an horrific earthquake in Tangshan, China, the biggest of the century, killed 250,000 people.

Back in Britain, it was the driest summer since 1727. While the soaring temperatures on the thermometer brought folks out in their thousands, and daily newspapers carried pictures of

crowds sizzling in the sun, hosepipe bans were introduced, reservoirs cracked and people were urged to turn off taps.

Politically, the heat was also on. Faced with growing political divisions within his cabinet and, outside Number 10, with rising domestic unrest, Harold Wilson resigned as prime minister, shortly afterward suffering a severe leadership defeat at the hands of James Callaghan. Elsewhere, things were even worse, with stars Jim Reeves and Perry Como fighting it out for the No. 1 slot in the album charts. Not for long.

The history books tell us that punk broke in 1976, but actually it was at the tail end of 1975–6; November, to be precise. The irate manager of a tiny upstairs room at St. Martin's School of Art thought that the band he had booked, The Sex Pistols, were too noisy. So he cut the power after only five songs. Eight months later, that same band had lit the fuse of a particularly incendiary art form.

In doing so, The Sex Pistols were inspired by, and in turn inspired, hordes of artists,

Right: (clockwise from top left)
Home computing becomes a reality;
Harold Wilson resigns; Mao Tse Tung
dies; Concorde launches.

Dr. Martens – The Story of an Icon

"DM's remind me of the Undertones in 1979 – good year, good boots, good drugs."

Alan McGee, owner of Creation Records, home to Oasis, Primal Scream and The Jesus and Mary Chain

singers, designers and other cultural experimenters. Punk also brought in its wake a wealth of new record labels, venues, fanzines and recording studios. Obviously, the most direct legacy of punk was the music. In early 1976, for example, two young northerners, both grammar school boys, were watching the Pistols in High Wycombe, in Berkshire. They drove home to Manchester afterwards, vowing to form their own band.

Taking their name from a headline in London's *Time Out* magazine, Pete Shelley and Howard Devoto formed Buzzcocks, a group whose brand of abrasive melodic pop introduced the world to such pop classics as 'Ever Fallen In Love With Someone You Shouldn't Have Fallen In Love With?' They also formed their own record label, New Hormones, which has subsequently been credited with being the first 'indie' record

company. When Buzzcocks debuted in Manchester supporting their heroes the Pistols, the crowd was small but enthusiastic; it contained, among others, Ian Curtis, Bernard Sumner and Peter Hook (later of Joy Division), Tony Wilson (who would go on to found Factory Records) and Steven Patrick Morrissey.

By mid '76, punk was gathering momentum and, with a headline-hungry media crowd now sniffing around the seedy clubs and sweaty gigs of the punk circuit, things really started to happen. The first punk record was The Damned's 'New Rose', only pipping the Pistols' 'Anarchy In The UK' to the post by a few weeks.

On the gig circuit, things were very much more active. The now-legendary 100 Club Punk Festival in London's Oxford Street, held on the 20th and 21st September, saw a first-night billing that included The Sex Pistols, Subway Sect and

Left: Pogoing punks at the Roxy in 1976.

Also in 1975

- Disposable razors introduced; catalytic converters unveiled.

- The first low-calorie beer, Miller Lite, is launched as consumers begin to educate themselves about diet and obesity.

- Disco fever stars to sweep the nightclubs of the world.

- *Jaws* is premiered. In the film, the shark-hunters bemoan how several hundred sailors were eaten alive by sharks when their boat sank – and how this tragedy prevented them from dropping a bomb that would have killed tens of thousands of people.

Also in 1976

- Martin Scorsese premiers his seminal Robert De Niro vehicle, the film *Taxi Driver*.

- Perrier sparkling mineral water is introduced for the first time.

- *The Muppet Show* launches on cable television, introducing the world to both Kermit the Frog and the redoubtable Miss Piggy.

- Eccentric billionaire and recluse Howard Hughes dies.

Michiko Koshino

"I chose to customize my favourite cherry-red Dr. Martens with my camouflage 100's print, as they are both classics."

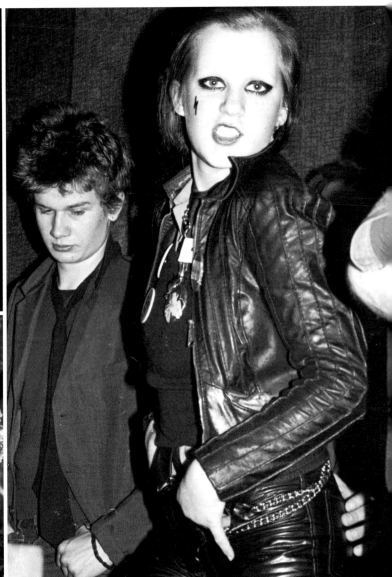

> "No other subculture illustrates more clearly the importance of theft and transformation in the development of style than punk. It incorporates conscious reference to the legacy of all preceding subcultures."

Helen Rees, social historian

Siouxsie and the Banshees. The following night saw the likes of The Damned, the Vibrators and Buzzcocks. The two-night event was infamous for many reasons. Sid Vicious, a member of the so-called Bromley Contingent, played drums for the hastily formed Siouxsie and the Banshees; some observers claimed that he invented 'the pogo' that night, by jumping violently up and down to the thrashed guitars. He also smashed a beer glass against a pillar, allegedly blinding a young woman in one eye.

The tabloid frenzy over this violence raised punk's profile by another notch. Yet this was nothing compared to the furore

that followed the so-called 'Bill Grundy incident', when the Pistols swore profusely on the early evening Thames TV *Today* show. The public reacted by jamming the television station's switchboard with complaints; the following morning's *Daily Mirror* front page denounced this latest group with the headline, 'The Filth and the Fury'. Amid all this outrage, it was ironic that The Sex Pistols were famous for not wearing Dr. Martens, instead preferring brothel creepers and biker boots or even trainers.

Now the floodgates of punk were opened. It was no longer the preserve of the London 'in-crowd'. Suddenly, the provincial kid could also be a part of something his parents detested. Despite the fact that punks were essentially doing

Left: Early punks adopted a stance of 'anti-fashion', wearing second-hand and customized clothes.

Also in 1977

- Elvis Presley dies on 16 August. Hollywood giant Charlie Chaplin also passes away this year, as do Bing Crosby and Groucho Marx.

- Terrorism rears its ugly head in Europe when West German police fight deadly and fatal conflicts with the Baader-Meinhof gang and the Red Army Faction – eventually Meinhof, Baader and his girlfriend die in their respective prison cells.

- The Son of Sam murders shock America – David Berkowitz, a postal clerk, claims he acted on the orders of his neighbour's dog.

- The Queen's Silver Jubilee sees street parties take over Britain's streets.

Also in 1978

- *Dallas* proves to be the television hit of the year.

- Disco fever grips the world.

- Over 98 per cent of US households now have a television.

- Keith Moon is found dead in his Mayfair flat after an overdose of Heminevrin.

"I hope I'll not be seeing you again."

Bill Grundy to The Sex Pistols after they swore on his TV show in December 1976, causing national outrage

much the same as all teenagers had done before them – that is, upsetting the older generation – it was not what they did that made the daily headlines so powerful: it was the public's rabid reactions. The establishment's horror merely reinforced the counter-culture potency of the movement.

The individuality of punk's ethos filtered into the fashions as well as the music. Just as DIY songwriting was the order of the day, so DIY fashion design prevailed. Hand-sprayed clothes and ripped trousers were the order or the day; irreverent home-made T-shirts were hand-painted or sprayed with provocative slogans, the latter often taken from films or books.

Sometimes, deliberately low-grade items such as string vests were chosen, which were then dyed in bright colours; alternatively, haute couture garments such as silk shirts were defaced, slashed, or filled with strategically placed holes. Safety pins, badges, patches,

Left: A Dr. Martens advert in the style of the Jamie Reid Sex Pistols artworks.

tape and chains were all improvised to make unique garments. Economy of style and price was vital. One interesting feature was the occasional (mis)appropriation of elements of teddy boy fashions, such as the ted's string ties or drainpipe trousers; these items were commonly adopted, much to the annoyance – not surprisingly – of the purist teds.

The availability of punk fashion, however, was extremely limited. In London, 'bondage' trousers were one of the staple items of punk's 'classic' look, and a select few punk clothing shops offered Londoners an array of weird and wonderful items. Elsewhere, there were no such outlets, and kids were forced to plunder Salvation Army and other charity shops for raw materials; thus, in the provinces, crudely painted T-shirts, mohair jumpers and tight trousers ruled. One item of punk gear that was available on a national scale, however – and at a uniform price – was the Dr. Martens boot.

It was only natural that the black DM's boot should become ↓

Also in 1979

- The portable Sony Walkman and the board game Trivial Pursuit are launched.

- Actor John Wayne, famous for his 'hard-man' roles in Spaghetti Westerns, dies; Earl Mountbatten, pillar of the British establishment, is assassinated by the IRA (Irish Republican Army).

- The Shah of Iran is overthrown by Ayatollah Khomeini, while the Soviets invade Afghanistan.

- Sid Vicious dies of a heroin overdose while awaiting trial for the murder of his girlfriend, Nancy Spungen.

- London police record only eight gun shots fired by their metropolitan officers in the entire year.

- The nuclear facility at Three Mile Island in Pennsylvania experiences a partial meltdown, causing the release of some radioactive material.

Kirk Originals

"Dr. Martens is a brand full of humour that doesn't take itself too seriously, which is part of its appeal. We wanted our boots to convey these traits and reflect our design ethos."

The Clash

Although punk lit the fuse for a generation of social, cultural and artistic revolution, some of the more refined musical minds found the guttural and fierce directness of The Sex Pistols rather unrewarding. Enter The Clash, for many, the greatest punk band of all time – more intriguing, more thoughtful and more complex than much of what punk's head-down thrash had to offer.

The band was fronted by the enigmatic and inspiring John Mellor, a.k.a. Joe Strummer, the son of a second secretary in the British diplomatic service. Born in the Turkish capital of Ankara, Strummer travelled extensively via his father's job and attended boarding school at the City of London Freemen's school in Surrey. After a short stint as a busker, his first band, the Vultures, made way for the rather more inspired pub rock/R&B of the 101ers.

His energetic live performances with this band attracted the attentions of New York Dolls' fan Mick Jones and art school student Paul Simonon, guitarist and bassist with the London SS, who promptly poached Strummer from the 101ers. Together they formed a new band, The Clash, and recruited Keith Levene on guitar and Terry Chimes on drums. Levene left after only five shows and would go on to join John Lydon's PiL, while Chimes lasted through the recording sessions for The Clash's debut album before trad-jazz purist Topper Headon took the drum stool, thereby completing what is seen as the definitive Clash line-up.

Many devotees regard The Clash's first official gig as having been the infamous 'Screen On The Green' gig, supporting The Sex Pistols. In fact, they had played to a small public audience at a London rehearsal hall some two weeks earlier, as well as at an unannounced gig with the Pistols in Sheffield. In the final month of 1976, The Clash supported The Sex Pistols on their fabled 'Anarchy In The UK' tour, although all but three of the gigs were cancelled due to public outrage.

With the spotlight firmly on punk, The Clash signed a global record deal with CBS. Shortly after, they recorded in just three weekends the fourteen tracks of

their eponymously titled debut album, penned largely by Strummer and Jones. The record was heavily championed by, among others, BBC Radio 1 DJ John Peel and its raging angst, fiery tempo and provocative social sloganeering made it a Top Twelve album in the UK – fuelled by the success of their typically inflammatory debut single, 'White Riot'.

"There's a million reasons why hippies failed."

Joe Strummer

Rolling Stone later went on to call this rough-hewn record 'the definitive punk album'. Not released in the US until 1979, the debut album meanwhile became America's biggest-selling import album ever, shifting over 100,000 copies.

Famous for their black ten-hole DM's, The Clash's style was as varied as their music was. Their trademark spray-painted boiler suits and shirts were paired with jackets and ties, T-shirts, black leather jackets, black shirts (often sleeveless) and even dog tags.

The Clash were not without their own brushes with the law, though these were perhaps on a rather more comical scale than those of the Pistols. In June 1977, Strummer and Headon were each fined £5 for spraying 'Clash' on a wall; the following week, the band were kept in police cells overnight for having failed to appear in court to answer a charge relating to the theft of a pillow case from a Holiday Inn.

November 1978 saw the second album, the hard-rock-tinged *Give 'Em Enough Rope*,

which scaled to No. 2 in the UK charts, failing to topple the *Grease* soundtrack from the top slot. Next up was 1979's eclectic *London Calling* (originally entitled *The New Testament*), regarded by many as the greatest rock album ever. *London Calling* broke the band through in America, where they played to massive arenas nationwide; they subsequently went on to support The Who in a tour of the US.

As the band evolved and punk's sharp edge faded, The Clash began to filter reggae into

"Everything I've ever said is rubbish. There's been the odd time where by pressure of numbers, law of averages, I've said something intelligent."

Joe Strummer, 1988

Dr. Martens – The Story of an Icon

their sound and an anti-racist rhetoric into their political stance. Ironically, much of the kudos attached to Strummer's outfit came from some of their less obvious punk statements, which included tracks such as 'Bank Robber' and 'Lost in the Supermarket'. Strangely enough, in 1990 'Rock The Casbah' became the first-ever record to be played on the Armed Forces Radio in the Persian Gulf.

This double album was priced as per a single album, a trait that the group continued – at not inconsiderable personal cost – with their sprawling third long player, *Sandinista*, which was released to mixed reviews. Inevitably, perhaps, some punk purists bemoaned this protracted triple album, claiming that The Clash had lost sight of the brevity and brutal essence that had originally been theirs and theirs alone. However, this was never an outfit that was going to rehash the three-chord punk sprint ad infinitum. Nonetheless, in many ways their commercial success was never as mighty as their critical acclaim. Prior to the 1991 re-release of 'Should I Stay Or Should I Go', courtesy of the Levi's advert, The Clash had never enjoyed a Top Ten single in their native Britain.

The album *Combat Rock*, from 1982, was tipped by many to be the prelude to US domination. Yet in many ways such success would have been anathema to The Clash and all that they represented. After the band split in the mid-'80s, Strummer went on to work on film soundtracks (*Walker*, *Permanent Record*, *Grosse Point Blank*) and even appeared in a selection of movies himself, including Alex Cox's *Straight To Hell* and Jim Jarmusch's *Mystery Train*.

Strummer's first solo album, *Earthquake Weather*, was met with modest applause in 1989. Then, two years later, he briefly replaced Shane MacGowan as the vocalist with the Pogues. In the mid-'90s, rumours began to circulate that the band had been offered £100 million to reform for a massive world tour.

But with Strummer's career now thriving – his band, the Mescalaros, were critically revered although enjoyed only muted commercial success – and talk of ongoing animosity between the founder members, the gossip remained just that, and the fanfare world tour with the celebrated original line-up never materialized.

Even The Sex Pistols' triumphant return to the live arena at north London's Finsbury Park in 1996 (for a multimillion-pound pay day) did not tempt the thinking man's punk rockers out of their retirement.

In December 2002, the shock news broke that Joe Strummer had died (the cause of death was a suspected heart attack). Strummer was just 50 years old. Only a few weeks earlier, the punk legend had been playing a benefit gig at Acton Town Hall in west London in support of the striking firemen of the UK.

Scott Henshall

"[I see Dr. Martens as] playing on the contradiction of strong, harsh and feminine."

"It meant that instead of thinking about doing it, we'd actually done it."

Pete Shelley of Buzzcocks on what punk meant to him, 1977

a staple feature of the punk aficionado's wardrobe, and it fitted in seamlessly with the prevailing thrift-store style. Punk's two defining fashion statements – short, badly cut hair and any trousers except flares – helped make the boot uncannily suitable.

The flexibility of style that was so much a part of punk might have limited the appeal of DM's, but the boot also proved to have scope for alteration – punk's confidence of spirit quickly saw many Docs being customized with unique designs. Malcolm Garrett, who designed all of the Buzzcocks' artwork – and, along with Jamie Reid, became one of the two lynchpins of punk design – vividly remembers embellishing his own pair of 1460s. Recalls Garrett, 'I painted my brown pair bright orange and silver, to coincide with the Buzzcocks' debut album, *Another Music In A Different Kitchen*. I had designed that album sleeve to be deliberately striking, very simple, clinical

Left: The Sex Pistols

even. I wanted my Docs to look the same, but I couldn't find any orange shoe paint so they ended up being red.'

Arguably, the Dr. Martens 1460 was the antithesis of what punk fashion stood for – after all, many punks prided themselves on being unique, non-uniform. In many respects, the 1460 was the only item of punk gear that was of a standard design. Up to this point, many had associated the boot with skinhead culture, making some punks reluctant to buy Docs; inevitably, though, the boot's durability and look reinforced its popularity.

Of course, there were dozens of other styles of punk footwear: the sling-back, the army combat boot, the brothel creeper, the monkey boot, even plastic jelly sandals and white stilettos. However, the 1460 was within the reach of even the most impoverished of punks. (In 1976 a pair of Docs still retailed for under £20, a fact immortalized in British performer Alexei Sayle's lyrical tribute: 'They're priceless, matchless, heat

resistant, waterproof, and retail for only nineteen pounds and ninety-nine pee.'). The boot's hard-wearing durability provided an additional economy.

Musically, there was little to tempt the youth of the mid '70s away from the bulging wave of snarling punk venom. In Britain, The Eagles had become the first group to achieve platinum status with their *Greatest Hits 1971–75* album, while the likes of Brotherhood of Man and Showaddywaddy dominated the charts. The increasingly angry' youth of the nation was left with alternatives such as Dana, Johnny Mathis, Status Quo or Alvin Stardust.

The introduction of FM radio had created a sonic world in which the newly christened Adult Oriented Rock ruled the airwaves. Prog rock raised its ugly head too, taking studio wizardry and technical virtuosity to new extremes, with bands such as Pink Floyd, Yes, Jethro Tull and Todd Rungren offering some of the best (and worst) examples. By contrast, while the US may also have boasted a fertile and creative punk scene, the social and economic scene on that side of the Atlantic was not as fractured as in the UK, so punk initially had far less impact than it did in its native territory.

"Give me a mandolin and I'll give you rock 'n' roll."

Keith Moon of The Who, 1977

Americans were listening predominantly to Led Zeppelin and other rock monsters, but also to artists like the blues-inspired Allman Brothers, or the country rock of The Eagles. In April 1977 The Damned became the first British punk band to hit the US, playing four nights at CBGB's. When they got to their hotel room, allegedly they found several gifts left for them by The Rolling Stones, including a birthday cake and seven meringue pies.

For all the headline-grabbing glory and pivotal, quite magnificent records, punk was quickly overshadowed in all but critical terms by a rising, more glamorous behemoth: disco. As with punk, there had been disco rumblings – though, unlike punk, the latter came from New York's dance floors – as early as the winter of 1974, while 1975 saw a veritable chart assault by acts such as KC and the Sunshine Band and Gloria Gaynor. The Silver Jubilee year of 1977 was punk's chart peak, in the UK at least; but even then artists such as Donna Summer were enjoying far greater commercial success.

When Elvis Presley died in August 1977, it seemed that much of Britain remained unmoved by punk. That week, Brotherhood of Man's 'Angelo' was at the top of the singles charts; Yes topped the album charts with *Going For The One* – the Pistols' 'Pretty Vacant' had only managed No. 6 the previous month. At least they had *Never Mind The Bollocks – Here's The Sex Pistols* up their sleeves, a chart-topping album in November of that Jubilee year.

By 1978, punk's bile was no match for the three-piece, white flared suit and medallion worn by John Travolta in *Saturday Night Fever*. This was Travolta's second smash film of 1978, complemented by the even bigger commercial success of *Grease* (the most successful musical film of all time), co-starring Olivia Newton-John. However, it was the white suit of *Saturday Night Fever* and the superb Bee Gees soundtrack (producing six chart-toppers) that proved enduring, and became so symbolic of the '70s. Oddly, while punk's critics pointed to its brevity in the public eye, Travolta's own musical heyday was equally short-lived – only a year after dominating the world's charts, he released a compilation album of hits from both *Saturday Night Fever* and *Grease*, which barely scraped into the US Top 200.

Of course, Dr. Martens sat oddly with the fleet-footed disco divas in the world of the mirrored ball; instead, strappy platform heels for women and platform loafers for men were all the rage. In the aftermath of disco having been catapulted into the mainstream, more manufactured acts, such as Boney M, enjoyed less credibility but quite breathtaking commercial success. Inevitably, disco, like punk, met with too much opposition; in this case, the 'Disco Sucks' campaign, and the writing was on the (coat room) wall.

One of the most striking aspects of punk is that despite the enormous impact it

Right: (clockwise from top left)
Rock supergroup Yes; *Saturday Night Fever*, **starring John Travolta; The Bee Gees in a still from their disastrous movie** *Sgt. Pepper's Lonely Hearts Club Band*; **the blockbuster film** *Grease*.

undoubtedly had on fashion, music, youth culture, art – and virtually every other aspect of popular culture – within a few months of its demise, it was deemed painfully unfashionable. The clothing, the style, the songs, the behaviour and the fashions were all abruptly discarded, almost without exception. Indeed, this ruthless slaying of ideas is typical of each new subculture, which has at its heart the rampant desire to destroy the past, and in particular the immediate past. However, one item, more than any other, seemed capable of surviving intact the demise of the punk phenomenon – the Dr. Martens boot.

Post-punk Oi!

As punk faded, it threw up various hybrids, including Oi! This mixture of skinhead and punk saw mohicans matched with Docs, skin-tight trousers, braces and colourful items of clothing. The name possibly derives from the Cockney pronunciation of 'hey'. Others claim it is taken from the Greek word 'oi poloi', meaning 'common people' or, more likely, from the Cockney Rejects album, *Oi, Oi, Oi.*

This fleeting scene, which was championed by the music press,

Above: A promotional poster for the Oi! tour. Right: Jimmy Pursey of Sham 69.

appeared to offer a new clarion call to Britain's disaffected youth, and was described by some as 'working-class punk' or 'real punk'. In the wake of punk becoming commercialised and sterile, certain purists derided bands like The Sex Pistols and The Clash for having lost sight of their original punk ideals.

Such doubters claimed that punk had been filled with middle-class opportunists, dropping their 'aitches', buying high-street punk clothes and temporarily dying their hair while that was the vogue. Instead, a legion of bands, many of whom had been around before, during and after the explosion of punk in 1976, led a fierce and at times brutal new wave of music.

At the forefront of this new, largely London-centred movement were bands such as Sham 69, Cock Sparrer and Slaughter and the Dogs. UK Subs, the Lurkers, the Ruts and Menace were also lumped in under this banner. Sham 69, led by the enigmatic Jimmy Pursey, were the leaders, and initially they tried to heal social divisions with songs like 'If The Kids Are United'. The Business were one of the other leading lights.

This new wave of skinhead-based subculture wore their ↓

Vivenne Westwood

"Tights protect and flatter women's legs. They give that glamorous touch. Dr. Martens boots are such a classic that there is no need to add anything to them, they are perfect as they are. The tights are used purely for that element of glamour and we have blessed them with a kiss!"

"The future is not what it used to be."

Robert De Niro in *Angel Heart*

Docs further up the leg, sometimes as high as 22 holes, and cut their trousers even higher so as to emphasize the boot. By way of contrast, they cut their hair very short, with the dark shadow and number one being dominant. Facial tattoos became popular, often amateurishly scrawled on the skin of the face with a blunt needle and a bottle of Indian ink (most professional tattooists refused to do facial work).

Many of these new skins carried with them an air of racial intolerance, violence and general thuggishness, which the old-school skins disliked intensely, not least because it discredited the whole skin scene. As a result, there were several battles between the two groups, including scraps on the celebrated King's Road in London, where older skins joined forces with teds to fight new skins and punks.

Unfortunately, the Oi! scene quickly unravelled due to growing scenes of violence. At many gigs by Peter and the Test

Left: Tattoos proclaimed the nationalistic bent of certain skinheads.

Tube Babies, security demanded that fans take off their DM's altogether, or at least remove the laces, just as the football police had done a decade earlier. Unwittingly, bands found themselves supported by increasing numbers of National Front devotees who infected many gigs with their racism and exaggerated tribalism. Jimmy Pursey was known to be extremely unhappy about this development, and at one Sham 69 gig where skins rioted, he left the stage in tears.

The Cockney Rejects attracted many football fans, especially with their Top 30 take on West Ham's anthem, 'I'm Forever Blowing Bubbles'. Other Oi! bands suffered a similar fate, including The Last Resort, the Angelic Upstarts, the Exploited, and the UK Subs. Yet this was despite the fact that many inside the scene felt that the media were over-emphasizing this violent minority.

A particularly vicious riot between Asian youths and Oi! followers at a 4 Skins gig proved to be the death knell of the phenomenon. By the end of 1981, the violence had

superseded the music and the Oi! movement was finished.

As punk's embers started to cool, James Callaghan, the prime minister of the day, faced his own darkest hour. The son of a naval chief petty officer, Callaghan was a former tax officer and TUC (Trades Union Congress) employee. A spell as chancellor in 1964 had proved disastrous when he failed to devalue the pound. Nonetheless, his rise through the Labour Party's ranks continued unabated, until he took over the premiership after Harold Wilson's surprise resignation in 1976. However, as prime minister he presided over yet another sterling crisis, which led to negotiations with the IMF (International Monetary Fund) for a rescue package.

Then, in 1978, came the 'Winter of Discontent', during which unions and local government workers in Britain exercised to the full their right to strike. As Callaghan's Labour cabinet struggled to cope with an increasingly powerful union faction, Britain was paralysed. Rubbish remained uncollected in huge rotting piles, crematorium workers refused to bury bodies, ambulances stayed at their stations. Bizarre incidents were recounted, such as that of a sick

"There are basically three kinds of people who 'perform'. There are those who do it naturally, those who want to possess that ability but don't have that touch, and there are those who want to and don't give a damn either way. I'm part of that last category."

Iggy Pop, 1975

elderly lady having been taken to hospital wrapped in a carpet by her worried doctor, who had bundled her into the back of his family car.

Ultimately, the economic strife brought Callaghan's government down, leaving Mrs Thatcher to win the March 1979 election and, in the process, to take over a country that she described as 'a nation that has had the stuffing knocked out of it'. Yet for many disillusioned voters – and as early as the following year – economic distraction simply turned to social alienation, when the first-ever woman prime minister seemed to offer little hope for the bleak futures of the younger generation.

By the end of the '70s, so much of what had gone before already seemed unfashionable, a pastiche, or just plain embarrassing. Yet the decade was in many ways a victim of its own evolution; the reason so many fads existed was because society seemed eager – anxious, even – to grab hold of anything new and exciting. There was change at every turn and most embraced it.

The fact that the '70s boasted so many disparate fashions, musical styles, TV shows and other odd pieces of cultural ephemera can, in hindsight, only be seen as positive, particularly in the light of what some have bemoaned as the more 'sterilized' society of the politically correct new millennium. It was a decade of strange haircuts, stranger clothes and outrageous music – which, when considered against the backdrop of such mayhem as fuel shortages, presidential corruption and modern terrorism, was no small achievement.

The '70s were perhaps the single most important decade for Dr. Martens, in the sense that these years reinforced and expanded the boot's place in the cultural lexicon.

A workwear item worn by a select few might easily have faded back onto the factory floor during this period, but these years saw Dr. Martens swap its reputation as a comfortable utility boot for the status of a full-blown cultural icon.

It is also worth noting that, at this point, Dr. Martens had never once advertised its product in anything other than shoe-trade magazines. Somehow the underbelly of youth had grasped the 1460 and dragged it into the cauldron of tribal subculture. The humble eight-hole boot never looked back.

Right: Dr. Martens advertising continued to play on the theme of the perennially popular 'bouncing' soles.

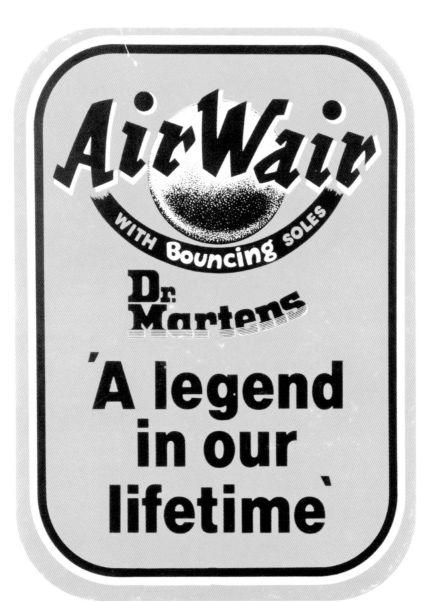

The Mohican

The Mohawks were an Indian tribe from Iroquois in New York State; the Mohicans, originally spelt Mohegan, were from Connecticut. Most frequently worn by the Omaha and Osage tribes, the long, thin plume of hair represented a line of buffaloes outlined against the horizon at sunset.

The Indians wore their Mohican haircuts as an act of defiance, daring the enemy into attacking them, and trying to take their scalps in the process. Their locks were often stiffened with bear grease or walnut oil, thus making the hair resemble the horn of a bull. The earliest known instance in Western Europe of widespread appropriation of the Mohican haircut was in France in 1945, when US paratroopers cut their hair in this style as a gesture of solidarity in the face of the looming jump across the Rhine.

In England in the '50s, Mancunian hairdresser George Mason offered the reward of £1 to the first youth who turned up at his salon and requested a 'mohican'. The winner, 15-year-old errand boy John Ross, was asked only to recommend the salon to his friends. Young Ross can comfortably claim to have pre-dated such godfathers of punk as Iggy Pop and Johnny Rotten by at least 20 years.

"No other subculture illustrates more clearly the importance of theft and transformation in the development of style than punk. It incorporates conscious reference to the legacy of all preceding subcultures."

Helen Rees, social historian

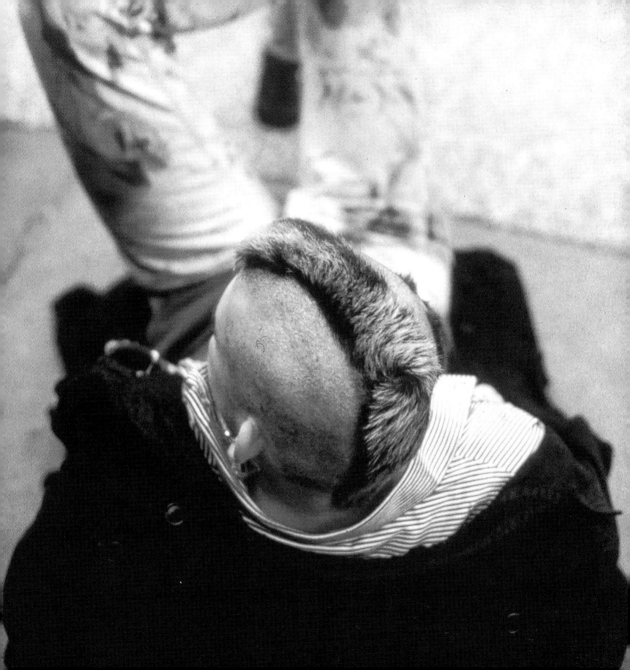

This was a decade of decadence, of money, of extravagance. It was all the more remarkable then, that it was also the era that saw Dr. Martens begin to infiltrate global youth culture. The latter was to prove an unashamedly self-deprecatory phenomenon in a world where glossy marketing and corporate greed were the order of the day.

80s

'80s

At the start of the '80s, the political permafrost of the Cold War was still very much an icy fact of modern life. With Britain in the hands of its first-ever woman prime minister and America about to elect a former actor, Ronald Reagan, as president, the winds of change were blowing fiercely.

Throughout the so-called Reagan–Thatcher era, a climate of 'greed is good' permeated almost every aspect of daily life, with the ethos of 'cash is king' dominating, and in many cases ruining, people's lives.

In America, Reagan was happy to announce that the Soviet Union was 'the focus of evil in the modern world', later on referring to the USSR as 'an evil empire'. The year he was elected, Reagan led a boycott of the Moscow Olympic Games (a gesture reciprocated in 1984 when the games were staged in Los Angeles).

In Britain, the tidal wave of nationalism, energized by the victorious war against the Argentines in the Falkland Islands in the South Atlantic, buoyed Margaret Thatcher's popularity in the polls to record levels. She encouraged every man and woman to become an entrepreneur, to buy their own house or the council's houses, to think big, to become self-reliant.

The explosion of computer technology was perhaps the biggest single evolutionary milestone of the '80s. By 1985, a microchip costing $5 was a thousand times more powerful than one that would have cost $100 ten years previously. The IBM personal computer, or PC, was introduced in 1981, followed by the mouse a short time later, while the Apple Macintosh debuted in 1984. Kids around the world squeezed themselves into tiny arcades to play games such as Donkey Kong and Pac Man, while home computers began to revolutionize schoolwork.

The business sector embraced the new technology wholeheartedly, and the subsequent globalization of commerce created millions of millionaires. The '80s brought us the chunky mobile phone, the sharp-suited City whiz earning six-figure bonuses, the 'power dressing' of shoulder-padded women's outfits or men's chalk-pinstriped three-piece suits, the essential Porsche 911 with its oversized whalefin, the 'power lunch' and countless

Right: (clockwise from top left) Thatcher, leader of '80s Britain; the miners who resisted the 'Iron Lady'; the fairy-tale wedding of 'Chaz and Di'; dismantling the Berlin Wall, 1989.

"Here is the stuff of which fairy tales are made."

Archbishop Runcie after officiating at the wedding ceremony
of HRH Prince Charles and Lady Diana Spencer

other symbols of this decade of excess. Life was all about flashing the cash and being young and upwardly mobile – the Yuppie (young urban – or upwardly mobile – professional) was born. There were beacons of selflessness, of course, such as Bob Geldof's Live Aid, but the dominant force in the '80s – the decade of acronyms – was, without doubt, the Yuppie.

Of course, this was all very well if you were the ones earning the money. For those on more modest earnings – or, in the case of the three million or so unemployed in Britain, none at all – this was salt in the wound of economic hardship. Mrs Thatcher would prove to be the longest-serving British prime minister for more than a 150 years, but her background as a shopkeeper's daughter did little to ingratiate her with much of the country's working-class population. In the face of high unemployment, Thatcher

Left: Mods reinvented, '80s style, in the spirit of *Quadrophenia*.

gradually strengthened the economy. In 1983 she won a landslide general election victory, bolstered by the wave of patriotism that followed Britain's victory in the Falklands. Her government then proceeded to introduce a radical programme of privatization and deregulation, coupled with tax cuts and sweeping reform of the trade unions. All of this was conducted against a background of high international profile and the fact of Thatcher being particularly close to Reagan.

Eventually, Mrs Thatcher's opposition to Britain's membership of the European Union contributed to her downfall, as did her ill-considered imposition of the Poll Tax and the brutal suppression of the 1984 miners' strike. Add to this famous conceits such as 'the Iron Lady is not for turning' and 'economics are the method; the object is to change the soul' (not forgetting the grand statement, 'there is no such thing as society'), and you had a recipe that many – particularly the young and less privileged – found obnoxious.

Scooter boys

One revivalist movement of this decade, which drew inspiration from various elements of previous subcultures, was the scooter-boy phenomenon of the late '70s and early '80s. This emerging cult figure had a passion for 'traditional' Rhythm & Blues, Tamla Motown, Northern Soul and adrenaline-pumping All-Niters. Like their modfather forebears, the scooter boys would gather at coastal resorts in their thousands and party hard for days at a time. As with so many youth cultures, drugs were used, with speed being a particular favorite.

These scooter boys sprang from the loins of a 1979 mod revival, which initially was quite purist in its stance. Soon, however, a small clique of self-styled scooter boys began to distance themselves from the mods. Many cultural historians are contemptuous of this new mutation of the mod, saying that this green-parka-wearing, scooter-riding new generation knew nothing of the original motivations and ethics of the early '60s mods. Their dirty parkas, covered with badges (not found on mod parkas; these

Lulu Guiness

"I wanted to add a touch of humour and femininity, so I changed the boots into a lilac Parisian house, just like one of my bags."

"Honey, I forgot to duck!"

Ronald Reagan – borrowing boxer Jack Dempsey's famous line – after being shot by John Hinckley in an assassination attempt two months into his presidency. Hinckley said that the shooting was a personal tribute to actress Jodi Foster

remained plain), and often anchored by a pair of gleaming cherry-red DM's, seemed a million miles from the sharp-suited predecessors of twenty years earlier.

However, scooter-boy expert Gareth Brown has suggested in his seminal book on the subject – entitled *Scooter Boys* – that the revival gripping the nation's youth in the early '80s was more complex than this, and that scooter boys were actually thoroughly schooled in the origins and essentials of mod. Says Brown, 'In the south [of Britain], the mainstay were from the mod revivalist school, while in the north they were more influenced by the ongoing face of scootering, the scooter boy.' It was the latter, more than any other mod splinter group, that adopted the cherry-red 1460.

As described above, the green parkas were frequently worn over faded denim jackets. The look was complemented by DM's, which were worn under ex-army drill trousers (often short). The DM's were in sharp contrast to the black-and-white bowling shoes of the mods, most famously worn by The Jam, and were in fact a deliberate ploy on the part of the scooter boys to differentiate themselves from such mod revivalists.

It wasn't just their choice of clothing that separated these scooter boys from the more purist mod revivalists. Their scooters also told a different, even more 'anti-mod' story. Unlike the highly chromed and heavily accessorized models favoured by the revivalists, scooter boys chose instead to customize the bodywork of their scooters.

Intricate airbrushed murals and cutaway panels were commonplace. They added extra-high bubble fly-screens, too, with a reversible flip-flop backrest. Black-and-white chequered mudflaps were also popular, and hinted at the occasional inter-mingling of this subculture with that of Two Tone. The Union Jack flag was also prevalent. Then, of course, there was the famed multitude of mirrors, plus the fur tail flying from the aerial.

At first, the two factions within the mod ranks were defined only by those in the know, within the inner circles. By 1982, however, the scooter-boy movement was idiosyncratic enough to define itself as such – the rally at Scarborough of that year was the first time that this new youth subculture had paraded itself publicly. By 1983, scooter boys were driven even further in their desire not to be mistaken for mod revivalists. So they ditched the green parkas and began wearing flying or leather jackets. Those scooter boys who still wore their parkas were, by then, something of a laughing stock.

One reason why this scootering cult is particularly pertinent to a history of Dr. Martens is that both phenomena enjoyed a huge international following. The scooter boys of the mid '80s soon began to find continental advocates championing their style – including the 1460 – with a passion. The first signs of this came with UK scooter boys' forays to mainland Europe for rallies at venues as far flung as Versailles, Barcelona, Vienna and Brussels.

Right: Phil Daniels in *Quadrophenia*, the classic mod movie, which was released in 1979.

> "Taste is a thin line. We sing about glue and all that. We feel that's within taste."

Johnny Ramone, 1980

Of course, scooters had been popular in Europe since the '50s, but this '80s revival was particularly strong in Holland, France and Italy. The scooter boys, travelling abroad en masse from the UK, revelled in the all-night bars, the red-light districts and the decriminalized soft drugs of, in particular, the Netherlands. German scooter boys were perhaps most influenced by the British fashion, and also looked heavily to the film *Quadrophenia*. This crossover into Teutonic youth culture was fuelled in part by large ex-pat contingencies of British builders and army personnel mixing with their fellow German scooterists.

This infection of Europe by the scooter boys provided a huge sales boost to Dr. Martens. On a more symbolic level, the dissemination of scooterist style and thought was analogous to the way in which the DM's boot

Left: A shoe from Dr. Martens sneaker range, first launched in the '70s.

has similarly seeped into European youth culture. Interestingly, the US scooter boys' movement was on a very small scale and, in the words of Gareth Brown, was 'more of a parody, a caricature' of the original look. Nonetheless, at this point in the mid '80s, the purchase of cherry-reds in America was a welcome, albeit small-scale transatlantic exchange that could only lay down solid foundations for the latter-day invasion of North America by Dr. Martens.

The youth cult

The start of the '80s saw Dr. Martens ruling Britain's schoolyards. In some respects, this was the era of the youth cult, with its bizarre mix of parkas, punks, mods, Two Tone, rude boys, and even denim jackets, inspired by the new wave of British heavy-metal bands. (DM's could occasionally be found in the headbangers' scene, although heavier bikers' boots were the preferred option.)

Also in 1980

- Ronald Reagan (ex-actor) beats Jimmy Carter (ex-peanut farmer) and takes up office in the White House.

- Former Beatle John Lennon is assassinated by obsessed fan Mark Chapman (for whom he had earlier signed his new album) outside his apartment in New York City.

- Post-it notes launched.

- The US leads the boycott of the Moscow Olympics in protest against the Soviet invasion of Afghanistan.

- Smallpox finally eradicated worldwide.

- Deaths of film maker Alfred Hitchcock, actor Steve McQueen, athlete Jesse Owen and comedian Peter Sellers (of *Pink Panther* fame, as bumbling Inspector Clouseau).

- 'Who Shot JR?' saga in long-running TV show *Dallas* rivets television fans worldwide.

"The music video might be the only new popular art form in American life."

Novelist Norman Mailer

Upgrading from your monkey boots to your first pair of DM's was a cherished rite of passage.

By contrast, thousands of kids across Britain felt genuine terror when confronted by the school bully towering above in his lofty sixteen-holers. Current AirWair Chairman Stephen Griggs was quick-witted enough to box around this dilemma: 'I wasn't a very tough boy, but all the hard cases left me alone because I owed them pairs of DM's. They knew that if they beat me up I wouldn't deliver.'

Yet, at the start of the '80s, Dr. Martens found themselves in an oddly paradoxical position. Although the 1460 was firmly ensconced in youth subculture and drenched in street credibility, it was about to face its most formidable adversary: the sneaker. Nike, the most obvious market leader, had debuted back in 1972, but sneakers can actually be traced way back to 1866, when Charles Goodyear produced the world's first pair. These were made with vulcanized rubber on the sole, canvas cloth on the uppers and cotton laces to tie the eyelets together. It was actually a sandal intended for use by rich society types for playing croquet and other ball games at the beach. The name 'sneakers' was a straightforward reference to the unobtrusive noise the shoes made when walking, especially when compared to the noisy clunk of the more traditional leather or wooden-soled shoe. The style soon caught on and became more affordable; Sears were even selling shoes for running in as early as 1897.

However, despite numerous styles of sneaker being popularized throughout the twentieth century, it wasn't until the late '70s that they became a 'craze' as such, a new trend that would enjoy seemingly permanent longevity. Magazines such as *Runner's World* started to enjoy huge circulation figures as the fitness boom of these years started to shift sneakers in vast quantities. Celebrities like Jane Fonda were all part of a new era of keep-fit. With the new popularity of exercise came the beginnings of the complex technology developed by sneaker makers. These more advanced manufacturing processes also set retail prices climbing – often well in excess of the price of a pair of Dr. Martens, though this seemed to matter little to the buyers of sneakers.

Faced with such severe competition, Dr. Martens did briefly toy with producing their own sneakers, even releasing a range called AirWair Sport; a mutated brand called WearAir enjoyed limited but short-lived success in the late '90s, too. However, it quickly became clear that the world of the sneaker was a parallel universe to that of the 1460, and one which would always remain at a distance.

The impact of sneakers was immense. Rock stars, film stars, skateboarding kids, commuters – at times it seemed everyone owned a pair of trainers (the average American had 2.5 pairs). White basketball boots provided a variation on the theme of the simple ankle-high running shoe and sold hugely well. Famous basketball players started to sign multimillion-dollar ↓

Right: Early Nike trainers.

Olivia Morris

"This is an Olivia Morris Dr. Martens boot. I have kept the essence and made it sexy."

> ## "People want art. They want showbiz. They want to see you rush off in your limousine."

Freddie Mercury, 1982

endorsement deals, Michael Jordan being the most obvious example. By the mid '90s, sneakers were an established fashion essential item, and accounted for nearly one half of all shoes sold in 1996.

The distinctive and unique Dr. Martens sole had previously been its unique selling point. When added to its solid and substantial construction, however, it unfortunately made the boot too heavy to wear for such sporting activities. Worse still, for skaters and the like, the sole did not exert enough hold to be of any use in gripping the board. Moreover, the strong point of the 1460 had been its durability and, although many sneakers could last years if looked after properly, the desire to remain fashionable demanded that pairs be replaced long before they became worn out.

Meanwhile, sneaker brands had become household names.

Left: Run-DMC popularized the wearing of trainers, specifically Adidas Super Star.

The boom in aerobic exercise classes, celebrity diets and fitness fads fuelled the sales of sneakers, such that companies like Nike and Reebok became mammoth global corporations. The social impact was matched by the cultural legacy, with songs such as Run-DMC's 1986 single, 'My Adidas'. That formative hip-hop act wore their classic white Super Star sneakers minus the laces, as seen in their video for the seminal fusion of rap and rock, 'Walk This Way', performed with Aerosmith.

The retail prices of sneakers rose so high that there were reports of robbery and even murder being perpetrated to pay for that month's must-have footwear. Pump-up tongues, air-filled transparent soles, flashing lights on the soles or heels, plastic discs for laces and a multitude of manufacturing processes and designs followed, such as 'octopus suckers', 'herringbones' and 'nubby cobbles' – all designed to keep

Also in 1981

- The US Department of Agriculture responds to cuts in the school-dinner programme by announcing in September of this year that ketchup may be counted as a vegetable.

- Official announcement of a new killer virus, initially known as GRID but soon replaced by the acronym AIDS (Acquired Immune Deficiency Syndrome).

- Prince Charles and Lady Diana Spencer marry – 750 million viewers remain glued to their television sets as the heir to the throne marries a 19-year-old former kindergarten teacher, a union immortalized in a million plates, teaspoons and teapots.

- Pac Man video game introduced.

- Pope John Paul II is shot.

- The US Space Shuttle makes its debut launch.

- MTV launched.

- Bill Haley, the father of rock 'n' roll, dies. Haley's hit '(We're Gonna) Rock Around the Clock', released with the Comets, had reached No. 1 in 1955.

> "No true skinheads are racist. Without the Jamaican culture, skinheads would not exist. It was their culture mixed with British working-class culture that made Skinhead what it is."

Roddy Moreno of SHARP (Skinheads Against Racial Prejudices)

the sneaker fan buying new pair after new pair. For much of the time, the gimmicks worked. Fortunately, Dr. Martens enjoyed their own exponential sales explosion in the '80s. Buoyed by their aforementioned adoption by '70s youth culture, the 1460 continued to find itself championed by countless subcultures through the decade.

Two Tone

The very first – the grim urban reality of Two Tone – had actually started seeping out of its West Midlands home in 1979. By the close of that year, punk's incisive edge had been largely blunted. Its death throes spewed up a myriad of musical hybrids and subcultural splinters, some equally potent, some much less so. Punk in its original form was left to dwindle into self-parody. It was old news, and kids were looking elsewhere for their teenage kicks.

For many, this came with the arrival of Two Tone. The movement found an unlikely home in the grim, grey Midlands city of Coventry, famous for Lady Godiva, bicycles, cars and the ferocious Second World War bombing raids that had razed its buildings to the ground. From the postwar rubble grew up a modern dystopia; the intention originally had been to revitalize the ravaged city, but the result was little more than a series of desolate grey buildings and large, soulless housing estates. The economic backdrop to 1979 added fuel to the fire of the already disaffected youth of that city, with unemployment high

and punk's rebellious but wilting chant falling on deaf ears.

One such suffocated Coventry youth was Jerry Dammers. The son of a clergyman, Dammers had first sung in a church choir. He was inspired to be in a rock band by seeing a televised performance of The Who's 'My Generation'. Dammers studied art and film and immersed himself in soul, funk and reggae legends such as Don Drummond, Desmond Dekker and Prince Buster. Then punk arrived in his town and everything changed.

After being thrown out of The Sissy Stone Soul Band for playing keyboards with his elbows (he was encouraged by some punks in the crowd), Dammers formed the Coventry Automatics with Horace Panter, brothers Noel and Lynval Golding and former punks Terry Hall and Roddy 'Radiation' Byers. Legend has it that prior to this, Dammers travelled to London to try to recruit a post-Pistols Johnny Rotten on vocals. Several permutations later, and the band's name was changed to The Specials. After dozens of cramped rehearsals in Dammers' flat (his keyboard was too big to be carried through the

Right: The Specials' Jerry Dammers.

"These children that you tastefully spit on have, for months, been spreading like mould on muck."

Billy Batty, *The Face*

doors), the band set about establishing their legend.

Their initial blend of reggae and punk proved unpopular with live audiences. On tour with The Clash, they found themselves the target of many an empty bottle (and several full ones) flung stageward. After this demoralizing tour, in the cold winter of 1978–9, The Specials began to formulate their masterplan. They dropped the reggae influence and made a sidestep to ska – the combination of this rhythmical vibrancy and punk's raw energy proved immediately explosive.

Signing a ground-breaking record deal with Chrysalis, The Specials formed their own record label, Two Tone, which was to provide the new movement with a spiritual home. London band Madness appeared

Left: The original Two Tone bands (from top left) Madness; Pauline Black from The Selecter; Buster Bloodvessel from Bad Manners; The Special AKA.

for one single (the tribute to ska originator Prince Buster, 'The Prince'), while The Specials' own Elvis Costello-produced eponymous debut album gave them a Top Five hit. The Two Tone record label would go on to have other releases from bands such as The Swinging Cats, The Friday Club, J.B. Allstars, The Apollinairs, the Bodysnatchers and Elvis Costello himself. (For the record, the eponymous single recorded by The Selecter in the shed of producer Roger Lomas is regarded by many as the very first Two Tone track.)

Other leading players in this latest subculture were The Beat, The Selecter and, of course, Madness. Other non-Two-Tone ska acts included The Tigers, Ska City Rockers, The Akrylykz, The Employees and The Pirahnas. These bands all thrived on the first wave of ska musicians such as the Skatalites, Baba Brooks, Ernest Ranglin, Laurel Aitken and Desmond Dekker. Indeed, Rico ↓

Also in 1982

- First liposuction procedure performed.

- The devastating effects on the environment of acid rain are recognized.

- Madonna's first single, 'Holiday', released.

- The Falklands War breaks out, and British troops are dispatched to the South Atlantic to liberate the British territory there from the Argentine forces laying claim to it.

- Steven Spielberg's *ET* becomes the biggest-grossing film of all time.

- Michael Jackson's *Thriller* becomes the biggest-selling album of all time.

- The singles 'Don't You Want Me', by the Human League, and 'Come On Eileen', by Dexy's Midnight Runners, are riding high both in the UK and in the US Billboard charts.

- A permanent artificial heart is implanted in a human being for the first time – the beneficiary is 61-year-old Dr Barney B. Clark in Salt Lake City, Utah.

Maria Chen

"This design was based around capitalizing on the recent 40th anniversary of Dr. Martens – by taking cutouts from newspapers and magazines, and also making even more memorable impressions of icons of the time, such as Madonna."

> # "This is our first gig in America, and we can't say how pleased you must be to have us here."

The Specials' Terry Hall introducing the band during their New York debut

Rodriguez, who played as a session musician in Jamaica and was trained by Dammers' hero Don Drummond, would later go on to guest with The Specials.

In September 1979, Madness and The Specials toured together and provoked a tidal wave of media and public interest in the developing movement. The previously reluctant music press jumped on board, and the exposure proved invaluable. Once Two Tone was heard nationwide, it exploded. Within months, it was the scene at schools, youth clubs, gigs, on the streets and in the underground.

Later, The Specials' masterpiece, 'Ghost Town', hit No. 1 just as Britain's inner cities ignited in a rash of rioting in Toxteth (Liverpool), Brixton (south London) and Handsworth (Birmingham). The song justifiably became the definitive snapshot of the times. It reflected the desperation of inner-city life, the poverty of many people in early Thatcherite Britain, and the dissatisfaction and frustration of those sections of society that were being ostracized by the Iron Lady.

This anti-establishment feel appealed to many in the skinhead movement, drawing them into Two Tone. Ska picked up on elements of the mod revival as well, so that crowds at such gigs were an eclectic and thoroughly varied mix, with black rude boys, white skinheads, mods, punks and suedeheads. This anti-racist element was a key factor; some fascist groups regularly incited fights at ska gigs, and The Specials' tour bus was once bricked as it drove past a group of neo-Nazis.

In response to this, Dammers and many of the key figures in the scene became involved in movements such as Rock Against Racism and, later, the Nelson Mandela Freedom Campaign. Dammers himself had experienced this scourge closer to home – an Asian doctor was stabbed to death in a chip shop opposite his flat. Matters were not helped by an often misinformed media; after a spate of violent stage invasions and racist violence at Two Tone gigs, the *London Evening News* ran a piece on The Selecter headlined, 'Don't rock with these Sieg Heilers'. This, despite the fact that only one of the seven band members was white, and that they were renowned for their anti-racist views and multicultural interests.

The ska scene

The grim reality of Coventry's housing estates was sharply at odds with the genesis of the Jamaican sound so loved by this new generation of musicians. Ska was originally a variant of the Jamaican dance music that had emerged in the late '50s and prospered in the early '60s Kingston scene. Originally, it was formed from a mixture of traditional Jamaican mento, jazz, ya-ya and Calypso, as well as some North American influences. This melting pot of music was played at dance halls or on the back of huge lorries carrying massive, ear-splitting mobile sound systems.

Ska historians point to Clement 'Sir Coxsone' Dodd (after the Yorkshire cricketer of

Right: The Rock Against Racism logo.

"Pop begins in bedrooms and ends up in supermarkets."

Damon Albarn of Blur, 1989

the same name) as having created the first ska tracks in late 1960, just a few months after Dr. Martens first started making boots (although any connection between the two was still a long way off). Before then, in the late '50s, bassist Cluet Johnson played his own brand of new music around town while greeting people with the phrase 'Love Skavoovie' – it is from this that the word 'ska' is seen by some to have been appropriated. Others claim it is derived from the sound of the hi-hat being opened and closed.

Ska was first imported into the UK via the West-Indian immigrant population. On arrival in Britain, it became known as blue beat or Jamaican Blues, and from these early incarnations evolved first rocksteady and then, in the late '60s, reggae. London enjoyed a particularly strong mid-to-late '60s ska scene. Many reggae stars started off playing ska, including Bob Marley, Bunny

Left: Poster for the film *The Harder They Come*.

Wailer and Peter Tosh, and they even sported cropped haircuts, a staple cut of working-class subcultures. As more skinhead Jamaicans (known as 'Cocos pelados') moved to the UK, the style caught on – an evolution that makes a mockery of the later fascistic skinhead movements.

As with so many musical or cultural movements, Two Tone had its very own distinct dress code. The origins of this were embedded deep in Jamaica with the rude-boy culture of the late '50s. 'Rude boy' was a term used to describe the subculture of frustrated, unemployed and often violent youngsters who roamed the dance halls earning an anti-social reputation in the newly independent Jamaica.

Some felt the label was justified; others saw the rude boys as being unfairly denigrated. *Melody Maker* once called them 'cool super-hooligans'. Jimmy Cliff played just such a rude boy, Ivanhoe Martin Rhygin', in the Perry Hanzell film *The Harder They Come*, a classic ska movie. ↓

Also in 1983

- The Green Party rises to prominence in Germany, but many people scoff at its environmental concerns.

- *The Thorn Birds* rules TV sets the world over.

- Apple introduces the computer mouse.

- Camcorders go on sale in the shops.

- Vinyl lovers the world over laugh at the latest fad – compact disc.

- Crack cocaine surfaces on the streets of urban America.

- The Soviet military shoots down a Korean passenger airline, Korean Airlines Flight 007, over the remote island of Sakhalin.

- Singer Karen Carpenter dies at the age of 32; her death is largely attributed to the 'slimming disease', anorexia nervosa.

Bad Manners

Another artist to spring from the fringes of the Two Tone scene, and one who vociferously championed Dr. Martens, is the inimitable Buster Bloodvessel, a.k.a. Doug Trendle.

Buster fronted another larger-than-life band, Bad Manners. Although many observers derided them for releasing such novelty hits as 'Lip Up Fatty', 'Special Brew' and 'The Can Can' in the midst of Two Tone's successes, the band had actually been playing ska-influenced music since way back in 1975, under the name Stoop Solo and the Sheet Starchers. Bad Manners were, in fact, once offered a deal by Two Tone, but turned it down.

Buster's literally enormous presence (he weighs around 25 stone, or 350lbs) was an awesome sight live. Aside from his frame, which was squeezed into large, dirty-striped T-shirts, he has a thirteen-inch tongue and is completely bald. Apparently, he also holds the world record for eating Big Macs – 30 in a row (he can reputedly fit an entire Big Mac in his mouth in one go). At one time, he opened a hotel for over-sized people called Fatty Towers. Sadly, it did not stay open for very long.

Buster's penchant for Dr. Martens is legendary. On one occasion, he was flying back to Britain for a performance on *Top of the Pops*, which he planned to do in full French can-can regalia. Unfortunately, UK customs officers would not allow him to bring his colossal bloomers into the country (they were, quite literally, 'something to declare').

So on arrival at the BBC's television studios, Buster had to rummage around the costume department for a suitable replacement. Then, just when he was about to go on stage, he was told he could not wear his beloved DM's. Buster said that at the time, 'It was like cutting off my feet.'

Buster and Bad Manners were once on Epic America, the same label as Michael Jackson. A curious combination, some might suggest. Says Buster, 'We couldn't figure out why they'd want a bunch of silly boys alongside him. It dawned on us later . . . we were a tax loss.'

Although Buster became ill on stage while performing in Europe in 2001, he recovered and, at the time of this book going to press, was still gigging relentlessly.

"I'm not sure when we will be out on tour again. Soon I hope. Depends if I am under the knife again or not."

Buster Bloodvessel, after collapsing on stage in Italy due to a severe hernia, 2002

Fake London

"I tried to reflect the spirit of other Fake product, which has always been based on recycled vintage cashmere in a mixture of heritage and modern punk."

"Crucifixes are sexy because there's a naked man on them."

Madonna, 1985

The culture drew heavily on a mixture of imported American R&B and jazz, mixed with various African elements.

Rude boys took great pride in their fashionable attire. This consisted chiefly of neat suits with noticeably short trousers, usually in two-tone fabrics. The outfits were anchored by loafers and topped by (optional) pork-pie hats, sometimes called 'stingy brims' or 'bluebeat hats'. When Desmond Dekker first came to the UK, his record company bought him a suit; Dekker immediately took a pair of scissors to it, cutting off the bottom six inches of each trouser leg.

Such was the fascinating backdrop to Two Tone's inspiration. This newer version was racially liberal, fun-loving and stylistically as much in debt to elements of mod culture as to Jamaican fashion. The Jamaican hats, dark suits and narrow ties did translate, however. Almost all of the early rude boys wore loafers – usually black – and

Left: Jimmy Cliff, the original rude boy.

their shirts and hats were often far more colourful than the subsequent monochrome style. In this, they were harking back to the extravagant tailoring of the Jamaicans, although predictably the style was toned down for the British followers. Rude-girl fashions often consisted of tight, knee-length skirts, often with zip-up sides, sleeveless shirts – usually one colour (black or white) – dark-red lipstick and shoulder-length hair. The uniform made for an impressive collection at any ska gig where the archetypal ska dance, 'the skank', was performed.

As the second phase began to grip Britain in the late '70s, there was one new addition to the wardrobe – Dr. Martens. Increasingly, ska and Two Tone were recruiting large numbers of disenchanted punks, curious mods and open-minded skinheads, and the boot began to stake its claim in this new subculture. The greying of areas between skins and ska was accentuated by the burgeoning popularity of the boots,

Also in 1984

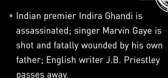

- Indian premier Indira Ghandi is assassinated; singer Marvin Gaye is shot and fatally wounded by his own father; English writer J.B. Priestley passes away.

- Band Aid aims to raise £72,000 to relieve famine in Ethiopia – after the follow-up Live Aid, Bob Geldof's charity declares that the mighty sum of £100 million has been raised.

- The film *Terminator*, starring seemingly indestructible tough guy Arnold Schwarzenegger, hits cinemas.

- Stone-washed jeans are launched.

- The first transplant of a baboon's heart into a baby is performed; the baby lives for another 15 days.

- UK band Status Quo announce they are 'splitting up' after no fewer than 22 years on the road.

- The South African religious leader, Bishop Desmond Tutu, is awarded the Nobel Peace Prize.

"Dr. Martens? I hate them."

Shane MacGowan

especially when worn with Harrington jackets with red-check linings, button badges and the occasional braces.

Also, some of the new revival mods who had first picked up on ska already wore DM's – Jerry Dammers himself wore many pseudo-mod outfits, including a '60s single-breasted mod suit bought in a second-hand shop, which provided the inspiration for a generation of Two Tone fans. It is ironic, perhaps, that a man famous for his gap-toothed grin should have become a fashion icon for thousands.

Furthermore, DM's seemed ideally suited to Two Tone's clean-cut, black-and-white image. The famous logo for Two Tone's record label was a character called Walt Jabsco (Walt, after Walt Disney) – a man in a black suit wearing black sunglasses, white shirt, black tie, pork-pie hat, white socks and black loafers, next to the famous Two Tone chequered pattern. This was a cartoon drawn by Dammers himself and based on Pete Tosh from the cover of a Wailing Wailers album. The shortened trousers made the importance of the right footwear even more apparent, and even the soles of Docs were two-tone! All of these factors compounded to make the boots a staple item in the world of Two Tone.

As a label and movement, Two Tone was relatively short-lived, with The Specials' line-up splintering off into various solo projects, the label struggling through financial difficulties and Dammers himself being locked in legal wrangles for years. Like punk before it, however, it had made an indelible mark on British culture.

Madness

From the ashes of Two Tone arose a band that would go on to become one of Britain's most popular acts: Madness. This was also the group that would do more than any other to endear Dr. Martens to British (and later American) youth subculture, winning over hearts and minds. In 1974, they had called themselves the Aldenham Glamour Boys, worn spray-painted Docs and imported Levi 501s, and driven ex-post office Morris Minor vans. When they came together as a band in 1976, they were initially called the North London Invaders, hailing as they did from the north London district of Camden. Evolving into Madness, the members were: art student Mike Barson and two former schoolmates, Chrissie Boy Foreman and Lee Thompson (who at the time were working together as gardeners); Graham 'Suggs' McPherson; Daniel Woodgate; Mark Bedford; and later, Cathal Smythe.

In the late '70s, their ska-influenced gigs garnered a small but loyal local following, although Suggs was once thrown out of the band for going to see a Chelsea football match instead of rehearsing! Then, one night at the Hope & Anchor pub in north London, they bumped into The Specials. Dammers and Suggs got talking, and crude and basic demo tapes were handed over. Support slots followed, including some superb shows at The Nashville, before Madness signed to Two Tone for a one-off single, 'The Prince'.

This was the first of a string of Top Twenty singles (21 in all) released by Madness between 1979 and 1986, making them one of the greatest UK singles bands of all time. Signing in the longer

Right: Cover of Madness album.

MADNESS *the business*

"MTV is the lava lamp of the 1980s."

Doug Ferrari

term with Stiff Records, home to Ian Dury and the Blockheads, Madness set about producing a series of inspired, eclectic, often darkly humorous and always delightfully catchy records.

First up was the single 'One Step Beyond', introduced by the now-legendary words spoken, not sung, by seventh member Chas Smash (alias Cathal Smythe): 'Hey You! Don't watch that, watch dis, this is the heavy, heavy monster sound.' The Nutty Sound had arrived. The album of the same name hit the No. 2 spot, despite the subsequent realization that most of Thompson's saxophone was actually in the wrong key! It was around this time that Chas Smash, who until now had only been recruited for his dancing and on-stage lunacy as Master of Ceremonies, was finally welcomed as a full-blown member of the band.

Accompanying Madness' quite superb catalogue of singles was a legion of unique promotional videos that made them a household name. Most famous

Left: Suggs of Madness – pioneers of The Nutty Sound.

of these was the clip used for the single 'Baggy Trousers', probably the greatest song ever written about schooldays. A recurring feature of these mini-movies would be saxophonist Lee Thompson dangling from a wire over the heads of the rest of the band. The band's biggest commercial success – but amazingly their only No. 1 hit – was May 1982's 'House of Fun', which also had a similarly madcap video.

In their long-form videos, *Complete Madness* and *Utter Madness*, they even went to the legendary A.H. Holts shoe shop in Camden to buy some Docs. Other bands who had become regular visitors to the shop included The Specials and The Beat. The office above was also home to Trigger Management, who looked after The Specials. Both bands would often watch *Top of the Pops* on the cheap television in the room above the piles of Dr. Martens in the shop below. Holts once sold dozens of steel-toecapped DM's to a Japanese clothes designer, who then proceeded to cut the leather off the cap and sell them for £200 a pair ... ↓

Also in 1985

- Mikhail Gorbachev becomes leader of the USSR after Chernenko dies. This event is seen by many as the trigger for the beginning of the end of the Cold War.

- British meteorologists confirm the existence of a hole in the ozone layer above the Antarctic; CFC (carbon-fluorocarbon) gases are blamed.

- British designer Laura Ashley dies.

- Rock Hudson becomes the first big Hollywood name to die of Aids-related illnesses.

- Wreck of the *Titanic* found; the liner had set sail on its maiden voyage from Southampton in 1912.

- Coca-Cola introduces the new Coke, which is rejected by the public and quickly leads to the reestablishment of the so-called 'Classic Coke'.

- The flagship of the Greenpeace environmental fleet, the *Rainbow Warrior*, is sunk off the coast of New Zealand by two bombs attached to its hull. The French government denies responsibility, but the ensuing outrage leads to high-level resignations and an eventual admission of complicity in the scandal.

Preen

"We were interested in this particular product, as Dr. Martens is a design classic and it was exciting to be given the chance to customize them. The inspiration for our idea was partly that of a Dickensian hobnail boot and also a beautiful version of boots a street urchin might wear, so they almost have a history of their own."

> "I'm glad to see The Clash have gone disco. It's about time they made some money."

David Lee Roth, 1981

Despite Madness' pop façade, they had to endure problems with neo-fascists at their gigs – in fact, they probably had the biggest skinhead following of all the ska-related bands. Although Suggs himself had started off life as a skin, as indeed had Chas Smash, the band grew increasingly concerned about the political preferences of some of their crowd and about the occasional outbreaks of violence. In fact, the single 'Embarrassment' dealt with the ludicrous reaction of a racist to a mixed-race child in his family.

Their final album, *Mad Not Mad*, which did not feature Barson, was crammed with classic tracks and tragi-comic observations (Suggs was less keen; he said producing it had been like 'polishing a turd'). Unfortunately, the album was recorded in an increasingly fractious atmosphere and in autumn 1986, Madness split up.

In the void left by the Camden Cowboys' absence, however, their reputation grew. Scores of bands cited them as an influence and their back catalogue continued to sell. In his last-ever interview before his assassination in 1980, John Lennon said that he greatly admired Madness. The most recognizable influence of Madness in global terms has been the debt paid to them by America's so-called 'third wave of ska' – namely bands such as No Doubt and the Mighty Mighty Bosstones.

Then, in 1992, the announcement was made that Madness was reforming for a (supposedly) one-off show at London's Finsbury Park, to be called 'Madstock'. The public response was so overwhelming that there have been several such reunions since. Indeed, in October 1999, the Magnificent Seven performed a secret gig at one of their old haunts, Camden's Electric Ballroom, in order to celebrate Dr. Martens' approaching 40th anniversary. Earlier in the day, a signing of boots and other Madness memorabilia at Dr. Martens central London 'Department Store' saw a queue of around 450 fans snaking around Covent Garden Piazza. Then, in 2002, the West End musical *Our House* opened to critical applause. Taking its inspiration from similar pop/rock-based musicals such as *Mama Mia!* (Abba) and *We Will Rock You* (Queen), the show was centred around many of Madness' hit songs.

In the post-punk, post-ska cauldron, Docs for once found few champions in British subculture. Soul and funk enjoyed an early '80s revival, and existentialist groups – clumsily and globally dubbed 'the movement with no name' – such as Echo and the Bunnymen did not often wear the boot.

Furthermore, the New Romantic movement, characterized by its extravagance and embroidered finery, also found little of interest in the simple, uniform minimalism of Doc Martens. The clique of disenchanted punk poseurs who led the New Romantics took their fascination with fashion to extreme levels. The Doc was rarely worn at New Romantic clubs like Louise's.

Right: An early promotional shot of Madness.

"Music is essentially useless, as life is."

George Santayana

Elsewhere, the short-lived 'casual' scene hailed labels such as Sergio Tacchini and Fila, whose over-priced cachet was the new fashion essential. With it came suede or coloured leather sneakers – almost useless for exercise purposes, but vital for all-important peer-group acceptance.

Across the Atlantic in the US, the underground development of a fledgling hip-hop and rap scene was only just beginning to make its presence felt. In time, this movement would become the most refreshing and innovative genre to be introduced to the music scene in years. For now, though, it remained a cult movement and Dr. Martens found no place in it.

However, all was not lost in the United States, where the 'infiltration' of the nation by Dr. Martens can actually be traced back to a time previous to the more obvious example of grunge. The Californian punk and hardcore scene at the

beginning of the '80s found a home for the hard-to-find boot almost a decade before its Seattle descendant.

Hardcore

Arriving hot on the heels of the punk scene, hardcore (short for hardcore punk) bands felt that the thematic and musical content of their punk predecessors lacked the depth and substance needed to sustain a genuinely ambitious social movement. Punk had hinted at a revolutionary stance and, indeed, in countless ways it had achieved exactly that – it had succeeded in turning the music, fashion and cultural world on its head. There had even been some superficial signs of this, with the use of swastikas (as sported, albeit briefly, by Sid Vicious and even Sioxsie Sioux), communist hammers and sickles or anti-monarchist sloganeering.

However, hardcore bands felt that punk's socio-political impact had fallen short. This concern was reinforced by the eventual mainstream dilution of punk into new wave pop-punk.

Left: New romantics, Nicola and Leigh Bowery.

Also in 1986

- Chernobyl nuclear reactor melts down in the USSR, sending up a cloud of deadly radioactive material, which drifts across Western Europe.

- The Space Shuttle Challenger explodes seconds after lift-off.

- Imelda Marcos' abandoned state residence in the Philippines reveals her collection of 1,060 pairs of shoes, but no DM's.

- When The Cure's Robert Smith cut off his goth locks in this year, MTV News broadcast updates of the 'happening' every half hour for a day.

Also in 1987

- UK shares crash on 19 October – dubbed 'Black Monday' – with falls that are twice as great as those that triggered the Great Depression in 1929. In the same month, severe gales wreak havoc across large swathes of southern UK.

- Pop-art painter and New York personality Andy Warhol dies; British hostage Terry Waite is freed from captivity in Lebanon.

"Music is but a fart that is sent from the guts of an instrument."

Anon

Underground bands started to form, christening themselves hardcore punk – both a reference to the more anti-establishment ideals they championed, and a moniker aimed at differentiating themselves from the more lightweight and commercially palatable batch of new wave, post-punk acts – such as Blondie – in the charts.

Sonically, hardcore pulled punk away from what had been – essentially – its '50s rock and roll influences, and obliterated the music with lightning-fast pace and sheer raucous noise, at times almost to the complete exclusion of what might traditionally be considered a melody. To the sceptical outsider, this was white noise. Yet these bands were often deftly talented musicians, and their angry yet compelling music made for a quite breathtaking live spectacle.

Predominantly based in Los Angeles and San Francisco, bands such as Crowd, China White, Black Flag the Adolescents, Dead Kennedys,

Bad Brains, Circle Jerks, the Outsiders and Social Distortion played hard-edged alternative music with a strictly underground feel. A few UK-based bands like Discharge followed suit, but the phenomenon remained a largely US-based subculture.

Hardcore US-style also differed from the punk movement in its fashion. Whereas some Continental hardcore outfits copied the leather jacket and extreme spiked haircuts of punk, American hardcore acts tended toward a more stripped-back look, invariably incorporating jeans and T-shirt with a shaved head.

This simplistic approach was the first rumbling of the so-called 'straight-edge' scene, which centred on the legendary band Minor Threat and its frontman Ian McKaye. This was a natural evolution of the original hardcore movement, and it expanded the music into an entire lifestyle by – effectively – preaching abstinence as a complete reaction to the

bacchanalian excesses of the old-school punks.

Naturally, both hardcore and straight-edge were vehemently contemptuous of the mainstream, so they went their own way – in the process, creating some of the finest independent record labels in the world. The most obvious example of this was Black Flag's SST label. When that band – led by Henry Rollins and Greg Ginn – delivered their first album to their major label, MCA, they were told that it could not be released due to its 'outrageous content'. Instead of toning down their efforts, Black Flag simply released the album themselves, and from there launched an independent label that would later boast such seminal acts as the Meat Puppets, the Minutemen, Dinosaur Jr, Husker Du and Sonic Youth.

Many of these hardcore bands toured prolifically, often visiting Europe on their travels. While in Britain, many band members bought Dr. Martens boots; after all, the boots were the perfect – and simple – practical footwear for their lifestyle and ethos. Inevitably, when these DM's were shipped back home after ↓

Right: Henry Rollins, the singer with influential hardcore band Black Flag.

Ben de Lisi

"I removed the hard-edge and replaced it with a 'Mary-Jane' sweetness."

> "Being seventeen and in a hardcore band is just about the pinnacle of experience."

Lou Barlow, Dinosaur Jr, 1987

each tour and polished up for US shows, the fans of the bands that wore them quickly started rooting out the boots for themselves.

At this point, however, availability was almost non-existent in the US; with the result that some hardcore bands even found themselves buying boots on order each time they played in Britain. Soon a handful of specialist stores had spotted this demand and began importing and stocking the boot.

Interestingly, in the light of future developments, as many girls as guys in the scene wore the boots. However, these early converts experienced the same problem as that endured by skinhead girls – getting hold of smaller sizes. In the mid '80s, Docs were especially popular with girls on this scene, although brothel creepers and monkey boots were also worn. It is worth noting that America

Left: Big is beautiful – but women often had trouble finding Docs in smaller sizes.

also had its own skinhead scene, which championed the boot, albeit in the wake of the initial interest shown by hardcore.

Back in the UK, the famous boots faced stiff competition from the emerging ranks of designer labels. The consumer excesses of the '80s heralded the arrival of 'label whores' on Britain's high streets. The humble shoe was not exempt from the prying eyes of a new breed of snobbish, brand-conscious consumer. Phrases like 'It's harder to climb the ladder of success in high heels' altered women's perception of workwear, and contributed to the archetypal vision of a besuited female rushing to the train station wearing a pair of white sneakers.

Once at work, flat-heeled shoes for women and classic brogues for men were the vogue. Away from work, destined for home and leisure activities, colourful and lightweight shoes such as espadrilles and jellies sold by the million. Even

Also in 1988

• Over 250 passengers die on board a Pan-Am flight after it is blown out of the sky by a terrorist bomb exploding while the aeroplane is flying over the small Scottish town of Lockerbie.

• Fax machines begin to appear in all corners of the workplace.

• Soviet troops begin their withdrawal from Afghanistan afer nine years of fighting – leaving the arena clear for the Taliban to take control.

Also in 1989

• The stealth bomber debuts, as do the marginally more frightening Teenage Mutant Ninja Turtles.

• The Exxon Valdez oil spill devastates wildlife after spilling eleven million gallons of crude oil into the sea near southern Alaska, slicking more than 1,000 miles of the world's most pristine coastline.

"DM's are the perfect lived-in footwear, an extended part of your soul, really. I wore my oldest pair to Reading Festival in 1997 and they were covered in mud. I thought to myself, 'This is where we have to split up, finally, after all these years.' So when I got back to my hotel room, I held a small funeral service and took some Polaroids of the boots, before I carefully placed them in the bin. It was like putting down a pet."

DJ Steve Lamacq

sneakers underwent a reinvention, with both Converse All Stars and patterned Vans (as popularized by the film *Fast Times at Ridgemont High*) becoming immensely popular.

Yet all was not lost for Dr. Martens. Indeed, the mid '80s marked the threshold of a fashion phenomenon that would propel the brand into the upper echelons of iconic global culture. Back on the seedy underbelly of youth subculture there were still many fragmented scenes worshipping the lowly 1460.

The most unfashionable (yet enduring) of all of these subcultures was goth. Spawned in the appropriately named Batcave club in London in 1981 and clothed at key goth shops such as Symphony of Shadows, the pale-faced, black-clad, doom-obsessed bands quickly garnered a large and cult following. Their unmistakable look spread across many countries. Although *Alternative Press* magazine hailed Nico's 1969 album, *The Marble Index*, as the first goth album, many observers looked toward the rise of Bauhaus or The Cramps, and other, later bands such as The Sisters of Mercy, The Cure, The Mission and Alien Sex Fiend.

Goth anti-fashion

The early '80s spark that would inspire a generation of goths was the distaste for the overtly commercial and unnecessarily frivolous fashions of the New Romantics. Goths, liked so many subcultures before them, were simply trying to subvert the norm; only in this instance, they took another youth culture – rather than the mainstream fancy – as the motivation for their counterpoint.

Cheekily, the Batcave club occupied the same venue as one of the New Romantics' essential clubs, which had the suitably frivolous name Gossips.

Right: Goths looking suitably gloomy.

"Conservatism is the worship of dead revolutions."

Clinton Rossiter

Of course, the women (and some men) on the goth scene often perched themselves on lofty stiletto heels; in tandem with this, the black 1460 also became a staple goth item. Goth has a peculiar ability to stay out of the mainstream, which is no doubt the reason why it has remained a subculture. While punk was consumed and spat out by a headline-hungry media and copied by a hundred high-street fashion stores, goth has stayed in the dark corners of its own making.

As has always been the case, certain individuals transcend such genres and attain their own legendary status. Thus Siouxsie Sioux moved on from her days embroiled in London's punk scene to become a heroine for millions of goths worldwide. Since which time she has formed the Creatures, along with Budgie, once more reinforcing her unassailable position as one of the unique subcultural icons of modern times. But Goth was not the only splinter group to

Left: From punk to goth – Siouxsie Sioux.

adopt the Dr. Martens boot. Psychobilly was another, even more unfashionable group that was ready to embrace the Doc.

Psychobilly

Deliberately perverting the rules of classic rockabilly, psychobillies merged that veteran subculture with punk's snarling menace. The original rockabilly had actually been a much more alternative and sexually charged musical fusion; but by the time Elvis had released numerous sugary pop travesties based on this original format, the edge had been dulled. Psychobillies dragged that essential essence back into the '80s, and twisted it to make something of their own.

The first pure psychobilly band were The Meteors. They started life in 1980 and were quickly dubbed 'mutant rockabilly', before the more fitting 'psychobilly' term was coined. With its anti-fashion stance, psychobilly upset the purists deeply. People crossed the road when a psychobilly approached – not surprising, given that he ↓

Doc Trivia

- The Griggs family once received an order from the Vatican for 11 pairs of Dr. Martens boots, including one pair, a size nine, in white.

- The laces in DM's have long had a colour code of their own. White laces on skins designated right-wing allegiances. Punks often preferred red laces, but these can also be worn to indicate leftist leanings. Lesbians often wear purple laces, as do goths. It is not known where or why these codes originated. Despite the trends, the codes were never universal, and people frequently had their own preferences, which were devoid of any political or social connotations.

- Dr. Martens have their own tartan, called MacMarten tartan.

- 'Vegetarian' Docs are made from a material often used on yachts.

- Through Dr. Martens, the Griggs have supported the Prince's Youth Business Trust, Shelter (a charity for the homeless), the National Youth Theatre and their local school – Wollaston School.

- Crack SAS troops wore Docs while fighting in the Falklands conflict.

Orla Kiely

"I have been a fan of the [Dr. Martens] brand for many years and therefore being able to design my 'fantasy DM' was a pure treat. I used leather that I use for many of my bags, soft but very durable. I removed the eyelets and placed my favourite fluoro pink stitching over the front dome of the boot. I am a colour fanatic and have teamed the pink with a pale leather for contrast."

"Aids kinda sucks, we ain't diggin' it."

was likely to sport a multicoloured quiff, bleached jeans, DM's halfway up his legs and a multitude of tattoos. Rockabilly bands like The Stray Cats and Polecats had enjoyed chart success in the early '80s during a sizeable rockabilly revival. Psychobilly, on the other hand, was far less commercial, far more punk.

Often covered in fake blood, The Meteors – led by Paul P. Ferech – were the pioneers of the movement, proclaiming, 'Only The Meteors are pure psychobilly'. The psychobilly mecca was the Klubfoot at the Clarendon in Hammersmith, west London.

The live shows had to be seen to be believed. Punters and bands alike would wear women's dresses, bleached jeans, Dr. Martens and kilts; the whole 'crowned' by enormous coloured quiffs and outlandish hairstyles. Members of the crowd would be pulled on to the stage and encouraged to drink vast quantities of alcohol, only then to be pinned on a spinning wheel and left until motion sickness and alcoholic over-indulgence produced the inevitable spray of vomit. Flour was also thrown over everyone present. Thus, at the end of a booze-filled, flour-dusted night, hordes of maniacal-looking psychobillies would head home through the darkness, looking like some fantastical nightmare from a strange B movie.

The scene swept rapidly across Europe, Scandinavia and even into Japan; for a few years it seemed as though every teenager on the underground had a quiff and a tattoo. It was a club for rebels. London four-piece The Guana Batz, fronted by Pip Hancox, were a colossal live proposition and grabbed themselves an army of demented followers. Other acts such as Demented Are Go and Batmobile were also popular. However, King Kurt were always the messiest! When word spread of their audiences throwing dead animals on to the stage, along with tins of paint and bags of flour, venue bans quickly ensued. Also riding high were The Restless, Demented Are Go, Torment, Frenzy, Long Tall Texans, The Milkshakes and The Sting Rays, with the cabaret provided by The Highliners. The music industry hated psychobilly – which just made it more fun.

Of course, Dr. Martens boots have always been about individualism. This was never more apparent than when they graced the feet of Paul King and his band King, whose image and music were completely at odds with the prevailing fashions of the mid '80s.

It was 1985 when King broke through. The same year, British meteorologists confirmed there was a hole in the ozone layer above Antarctica; Rock Hudson became Hollywood's first big-name casualty to die of Aids; Greenpeace's *Rainbow Warrior* was bombed by French agents; and the Rock and Roll Hall of Fame in Cleveland, Ohio, was inaugurated. Mainstream music gave us Whitney Houston's self-titled debut album and Dire Straits' *Brothers In Arms*. Yet back in Coventry, half a decade after Two Tone, one band, the brainchild of lead singer Paul King, was surfacing that would change the face of Dr. Martens boots forever.

King hit the No. 2 spot early in 1985 with the single 'Love And Pride'. Paul King had been a 12-year-old suedehead fascinated by Bowie, glam and then Two

Right: Psychobillies 'relaxing' together.

'Tonight we are armpit deep in broken glass, solidifying sweat and brain-dead soulless psychobillies with tattoos on their foreheads and bloodlust in their eyes all hunting for live brains to nourish their rotting flesh as every horror in London assembles. Things quickly get out of hand as huge evil mutant flat-top monsters take over the dance floor to wrench and claw at each other in the terrifyingly violent ritual of rockabilly dancing. I try fighting my way down the front but I'm beaten back by a hideously malevolent deathwalker messily devouring a weaker victim.

"Back, you evil spawn of hell," I scream, "You are blocking my view of the lead guitarist." I clutch my crucifix but against these creatures it is of little use. A few, the dim light of proto-intelligence shining feebly in their eyes, battle with equally foul bouncers and intestines fly in the ensuing carnage as more zombies pile on top, naked flesh gleaming with raw blood and splattered human remains. I am backed into a corner and resolve to sell my life dearly. Four of the creatures start eating my girlfriend.

"Don't kill her," I protest. "She is paying my bus fare home."

Mercifully the gig ends and the walking dead shuffle off, shoulders hunched, flesh dribbling from mouths. I find I am limping. One of my feet has been bitten off. Never mind, it's a small price to pay. The Guana Batz were fab.'

Review of Guana Batz gig at the Klubfoot by fiction author Martin Millar in the *NME*   Right: Pip of the Guana Batz

> # "To get anywhere in life, you have to be anti-social. Otherwise you will end up getting devoured."

Sean Connery

Tone. After his previous band, The Reluctant Stereotypes, split up, he formed King. The band struggled with their first three singles (including one called 'Sole On My Boot') before 'Love And Pride' broke through. Their manager, Perry Haines, later went on to found and edit the seminal fashion publication *i-D* magazine.

King's fashion sense was a unique blend of skinhead and glam. Wearing short trousers, long, quiffed hair and large boots, King himself called the unique hybrid a 'psychedelic skin look' or 'multi-tone', as opposed to two-tone. He was fascinated by the *Clockwork Orange* look, and was heavily influenced by Bowie, whose own Ziggy Stardust project had also been highly affected by that film.

The band's chief trademark, however, were their multi-coloured Dr. Martens. Each

Left: Paul King with his band King appears on *The Tube* sporting a pair of his favourite Dr. Martens.

television performance saw them appear with different-coloured boots on their feet – indeed, the 'Love And Pride' video featured the band and dozens of kids spraying their boots in an array of colours. Often, King's Docs were also decorated, with straps across the laces, buckles, patent leather and, in one instance, hand-painted with a portrait of the singer.

The boots became such a feature of King's success that AirWair approached the band, who were subsequently given several pairs (including one with flashing lights on the sole!). British teen magazine *Smash Hits* reflected Paul King's heart-throb status by running a feature headlined 'How To Paint Your DM's Like King', while style bible *The Face* also featured the band's music and footwear. When the band appeared on *Top of the Pops*, King wore a custom-made gold pair.

Paul King himself had seen coloured Docs way back in 1974.

'I first saw them at football matches. When Coventry played Chelsea, the London skins were into Bowie and called themselves Bowie Bootboys. They wore big DM's painted in Chelsea blue.' In many ways, King's championing of the boot was the first time that DM's had achieved a celebrity status that was totally devoid of violence. Add to this King's sex appeal, and suddenly the boots were exposed to a new generation (and gender) of wearers.

The fact that girls were now buying Dr. Martens was only spotted as a trend after AirWair noted a large increase in the sales of boys' sizes – realizing later that this was actually evidence of girls purchasing the smaller boot.

King disbanded abruptly in 1986 after two excellent but underrated albums. Legend has it that one evening on tour, Paul King met J.J. Burnel of the Stranglers, famous for his all-black look and black 1460s. They spotted each other across the bar. Burnel approached King and said, 'So, you're the one who wears those multi-coloured DM's – I think they should always be black myself.'

King were not the only band to wear DM's in the '80s. Also often seen in Dr. Martens was Martin ↓

Rude

"Dr. Martens are wheeely bootiful! And we've revamped them for the new millennium."

"If it's mumbled garage you want, you've come to the right place."

John Langford of The Mekons, 1985

Gore of Depeche Mode. There are few bands who have been so complex, vital and innovative – and yet successful – as Depeche Mode. This Essex band, formed out of schoolboy friendships and a love of alternative music, produced album after album of quite inspirational music. Their own take on the industrial scene, their groundbreaking use of technology and simply breathtaking live shows has taken stadium music to a new level. Mammoth tours, taking in all corners of the globe, have transformed them over the years from a relatively lightweight British pop band into a multi-faceted, multi-layered rock behemoth. Furthermore, their presentation has always been impeccable, with the majority of their instantly identifiable videos and art photography being taken by the legendary photographer Anton Corbijn.

Their on-tour difficulties and Dave Gahan's much-publicized battles with health problems have often been overly emphasized by the media, but these difficulties should not be allowed to obscure the fact that Depeche Mode are one of the biggest and most creative bands of all time. At the epicentre of this unique creativity is the songwriting genius of Martin Gore, who often wore a gold pair of sixteen-eyelet DM's on tour.

Another such act – and arguably the finest band of that period – was The Smiths, whose lead singer Morrissey frequently wore both the shoe and the boot. Morrissey's fans wore similar clothes, and mimicked his trademark quiff religiously. Along with King, this was another early example of girls wearing DM's, perhaps for the first time.

The Smiths generated a cult following that has rarely been equalled in British music, and their slew of brilliant singles rejuvenated a rather tired and unimaginative British music scene. Since his solo career was launched, Morrissey has enjoyed more global success than the Smiths ever achieved.

Morrissey's guitarist, Boz, recalls with relish his early days in music: 'As precocious teenagers, we rebelled against the staid teddy-boy image and fashion of crepe shoes and drape suits by wearing regulation council-issue donkey jackets, lumberjack shirts, turned-up Levi's and DM's, sometimes with steel toecaps, sometimes exposed, which would also come in handy during the odd scrap with Neasden skins. Then later, during the early Polecats shows, we used to jump around like epileptic grasshoppers and DM's were the only shoe to grip well on any stage surface, covered with any amount of beer and bodily fluids.'

The Cure, who had formed back in 1978 around the central genius of Robert Smith, did not actually wear DM's; members preferred pointed suede boots or, in Smith's case, oversized tongues on white basketball boots. However, Simon Gallup on bass frequently wore knee-high Docs.

The tail end of the '80s saw a rash of bands from the Midlands town of Stourbridge burst onto the music scene. The first grebos were Pop Will Eat Itself, led by the enigmatic Clint Mansell, whose pillar-box-red

Right: Depeche Mode; the original line-up with Vince Clarke.

"I'm from Stourbridge. It's no big deal. Everyone's got to come from somewhere, sir."

PWEI's Clint Mansell when questioned about the 'Stourbridge scene'

dreadlocks and compelling stage presence made him an unforgettable frontman. Even the word 'grebo' was taken from a Pop Will Eat Itself song. Ned's Atomic Dustbin and The Wonder Stuff were the other two key bands; again, most of their members were from around Stourbridge. All three Midlands' bands quickly won over legions of fans with their relentless gigging and snappily titled albums, such as *The Eight Legged Groove Machine*.

This author even wrote his first book about that trio of acts, calling it *The Eight Legged Atomic Dustbin Will Eat Itself*. No publishers would commit themselves to printing the book, yet the strength of the scene on the underground meant that over 7,500 self-printed copies were sold simply by standing outside gigs with plastic carrier bags full of books and sweat-soaked cash.

Left: None blacker. Tousle-topped goths The Cure.

The media latched onto this scene and in no time threw other bands and characters in the grebo pot – the sample-obsessed duo, Carter the Unstoppable Sex Machine, the brilliant songwriting of Wiz from Mega City Four, the angry yet musically deft releases of The Senseless Things. Although all of these bands were sonically diverse, the loosely based movement and its thousands of fans dominated the British alternative music scene for two years. The standard choice of footwear was almost exclusively Dr. Martens, with the accompanying loud, sloganeering band T-shirts selling in their thousands.

Reinvention

Away from the world of music and fashion, the '80s were a pivotal decade in late twentieth-century history. The glamour and glitz of TV shows such as *Dynasty* and the emergence of a modern celebrity culture served, unfortunately, only as minor

distractions from some terrible events worldwide. These ten years saw their fair share of horror. In 1984, 3,500 people were left dead and 200,000 injured after the leaking of a lethal gas from the Union Carbide pesticide plant in Bhopal, India; the same year, a harrowing and unrelieved famine resulted in the deaths of starving millions in sub-Saharan Africa. Only two years later, a Soviet nuclear reactor in Chernobyl exploded, spreading a cloud of radioactive dust across much of Europe.

Even humankind's positive progress was tainted by death and disaster: the first Space Shuttle blasted off on 12 April 1981; five years later, seven astronauts were killed when the US Space Shuttle Challenger exploded exactly 73 seconds after take-off.

Politically, however, away from the dole queues and fragile housing and stock markets, there was cause for hope. Whereas previously Reagan had demonized the Soviets, ten years later so much had changed. The Berlin Wall was brought down in 1989 – a vivid symbol of the final collapse of communism and the signal for the opening-up of diplomatic dialogue between two former rival superpowers.

"Jangly guitars do not my plonker pull."

Billy Duffy of The Cult, 1987.

Europe seemed to reinvent itself almost overnight, although such liberation was the expression of cumulative years of social and economic unrest at the hands of oppressive Eastern Bloc rulers. The crock of gold at the end of the rainbow was never going to be entirely without consequence, of course; later conflicts in Serbia and other equally unstable parts of Europe would be testimony to that. But for now, there was a genuine celebratory atmosphere infecting most of the Continent. This truly was a socio-political metamorphosis; a positive step brought into heightened relief by the intransigently brutal fist still ruling China. There, the regime was responsible for the crushing of pro-democracy demonstrators in the Tiananmen Square Massacre in 1989.

Similarly, but on a much more microcosmic scale, parts of the previously reviled skinhead movement were attempting to redefine what it was to be a skinhead, and what such a lifestyle represented. The inescapable fact was that over

the years the look had become associated with violent racists. And, inescapably, Dr. Martens was a key part of that image. The mutation of the original skinhead values into the tabloid-scaring, violent beast that became the archetype led to a counter-culture that fought to highlight this betrayal.

Many of the latter's members had suffered at the hands of society or the police for their style, in spite of their liberal views. For example, skinhead folklore suggests that in one British town during the late '70s, individuals with cropped haircuts were banned from going out of their houses after 10 p.m., on pain of arrest. This was not confined to Britain, either; regular revivals of skinheads have spread the culture to other countries and parts of the world – France, Germany, Australia, America, South America and, after the collapse of communism, Czechoslovakia and Hungary, all of which have large skinhead populations.

The '70s, more than any other decade, witnessed the greatest

problems with neo-Nazis and skinhead groups in the UK, whom non-racist skins often call 'boneheads'. Spearheading the musical branch of this anti-Nazi skinhead movement was the trio The Redskins. Once called No Swastikas, The Redskins united the left-wing skinhead movement with their brash, often belligerent and ranting punk hybrid. Lead singer Chris Dean, himself a writer for *NME*, renamed himself X. Moore. His lyrics were highly politicized, and gigs saw the band members berate fascists and right-wing political sympathizers with energy. Indeed, all three were members of the Socialist Workers' Party.

Although they split up in 1986, The Redskins were just one strong example of the growing tide of anti-fascist feeling within the skinhead movement. Concerts by the Anti-Nazi League and Rock Against Racism have proved similarly potent in fighting this menace. Jerry Dammers, formerly of The Specials, was at the forefront of this phenomenon. He helped organize two of the finest examples of such politically ↓

Right: (clockwise from top left) Challenger explodes; Bhopal chemical spill; Tiananmen square; Chernobyl.

Wale Adeyemi

"UK street meets US bling in an Adeyemi culture clash."

Red Or Dead

One of the key figures in the evolution of Dr. Martens into the iconic brand it is today is maverick designer Wayne Hemingway.

Although he is now a highly esteemed architectural designer, Hemingway's origins lie firmly in the fashion underground. In 1982 he founded the influential Red Or Dead label, and since then has established himself as one of the UK's most prominent designers of modern times. The role of Dr. Martens in that success is pivotal.

Hemingway was born in 1961 in the typical British seaside town of Morecambe, in the north of England, where his Red Indian father – Billy Two Rivers – was a wrestler on the pier. As a child, he can recall his mother and grandmother dressing him up as Elvis, one of The Beatles or even Tarzan. As he grew older, Hemingway immersed himself in a variety of fashions as each new trend came along, including northern soul, punk, disco, new romantic and rockabilly. Yet it was his early penchant for glam rock and, in particular, the band Slade that introduced Hemingway to Dr. Martens – an event that would irrevocably alter the course of his life.

In a one-to-one interview with this author, Hemingway mused, 'I did wear Dr. Martens as a young kid. My first experience of them was in 1972 as an 11-year-old lad going to watch Blackburn Rovers. I wore my skinhead trousers, Harrington jacket and feather haircut, complete with cherry-red 1460s, thinking I was this big lad. I used to buy the boots from army surplus stores or from a place in Blackburn called Tommy Balls, which used to get seconds. There didn't seem to be any of the more traditional shoe retailers stocking DM's at that point. When we got to the gates of Ewood Park [the football ground], I recall vividly being asked to hand over the laces – a regular occurrence to prevent the hooligans from kicking people. I couldn't believe it, I was only eleven, I was the last person who was ever going to kick anybody. The police told me I'd get my laces back at the end of the match but obviously I never did. I trudged home really upset because I had to walk all the way back into Blackburn, which was a bloody long walk that wasn't made any easier because of my boots. They were too big for me anyway and without laces it was tough for an 11-year-old. I was also so worried that my mum would think of me as a football hooligan. For the most part, I wore them as a Slade fan; you didn't go around in platforms, you wore DM's.

'I don't think I wore them again until that whole Echo and the Bunnymen scene. Fans of those sorts of bands would wear Chinese slippers and long overcoats in the summer and black 1460s in the winter. It was

Right: Red Or Dead shoes.

very much an agitprop, radical revolutionary Russian look. That brought Dr Martens back into the forefront of my mind in the early '80s.'

It was around this time that Hemingway moved to London to study for a degree. There, he formed a band. In a desperate attempt to raise funds for the band, Hemingway one day decided to empty his wardrobe – and that of his childhood sweetheart (now wife Gerardine) – and take the contents to north London's famous Camden Market, where he had an idea he could sell them. Thus were sown the roots of Red Or Dead.

From day one, his and Gerardine's goal was to break down the elitist barriers that characterized the designer fashion industry. 'We'd like to think that we played a part in removing the stigma from shopping for cool stuff on the high street.' By the end of the first year, they were running sixteen stalls, with shipments of second-hand clothing and footwear being brought in from all over the world. Absolutely central to this whole burgeoning empire was the Dr. Martens boot.

The Red Or Dead connection with working-class clothing was not confined to the couple's relationship with Dr. Martens.

The very first Red Or Dead collection was inspired by Russian peasant clothing – it proved an immediate success, triggering orders from Macy's department store in New York. Yet it was the simple 1460 that lay at the very heart of Wayne's meteoric success. He recalls how the crucial relationship with DM's developed: 'In the early '80s, when Red Or Dead was establishing itself, the main look of the moment was that of a designer called Azzedine Alaii, based in Paris. He was quite hallowed in fashion circles. His look was called "Other Body Conscious Look", which consisted of a black, tight-fitting, sexy dress in lycra, very much like the women wore in the Robert Palmer video for "Addicted To Love". At the end of this dress they would wear a fuck-off pair of black stilettos. This look was appealing right across the board, [to] young trendies as well as fashion groupies.

'What we did at Red Or Dead was subvert that look with a big pair of boots instead of stilettos. The reason I chose Dr. Martens was simply because of my knowledge of the brand from when I was younger. We did a photo shoot – an advert – for a magazine and showed the same

images in one of our shops and it just went absolutely mental. It just took off! Every magazine from high fashion to *Just 17* wanted to talk about Dr. Martens and this body-conscious look.

'In twenty years within the fashion industry, I have never known a phenomenon that has gone round the world at the speed that this did. Within months, we had opened stalls all over. It was incredible. We would be offloading our vans at first light at these markets, particularly Camden, and there would already be queues of these really attractive girls waiting there, "Have you got a size five?" It was mostly size fives or five and a half. Up until this point, Dr. Martens had been a predominantly male brand, so the Griggs' factories just weren't really geared up to making such quantities of smaller sizes. So the rarity added even more kudos – the smaller sizes were as rare as rocking-horse shit.

'I would go round touring every single old-fashioned footwear wholesaler in the country looking for DM's, absolutely everywhere. We'd buy everything from all the factories and army surplus shops – thin

Right: Wayne and Gerardine Hemingway.

soles, thick soles, whatever they had, we cleaned them out. They were selling these boots for £15 and I would sell them on for £30. Next thing we knew it had gone global. The first places it really transferred to were France and Japan. But we controlled it very, very carefully, to keep it cool, which was key. We only sent pairs to really trendy shops abroad. We restricted supply where possible and stayed away from garish patterns and colours. This kept it rare, so much so that back in the UK tourists would come to the stalls with great big army kit bags on their back and order sheets for their friends and families, coming out with big wads of cash. It was a total licence to print money.

'Next we opened a little shop in Soho and the first fashion shop in Neal Street, Covent Garden. The stalls – and later shops – sold a mixture of early Red Or Dead clothing, second-hand clothing, retro canvas and Dr. Martens. We'd have staff cutting the toes out of Dr Martens – something that Patrick Cox also did, although I don't know who was first – customizing on demand, and the cost of that work would be their wages. This success naturally evolved onto the catwalk – our

first catwalk collection contained the famous 'Space Baby' Dr. Martens boot, which is a rare collector's item nowadays, fetching upward of £500 or more at auction.

'It provided a healthy fund – that money coming in for selling those DM's we boxed up in a bloody big lock-up in Wembley. It was a great source of income. We got a good five or six years from that and you can bank a lot of money in that time.'

A maverick himself, Hemingway is drawn constantly toward unorthodox stories and characters. One of his favourite English eccentrics, Stanley Green, used to make a daily pilgrimage up and down London's Oxford Street, bearing a placard with the legend 'Eat Less Protein'.

'Stanley Green was the old man who used to walk down Oxford Street with a big placard claiming that protein was the root of evil,' says Hemingway. 'I used to love seeing him and really liked his bits of political activism. He was about as much "street" as you can possibly get, as well as a prime example of English eccentricity.'

Subsequently, Red Or Dead's 1993 collection immortalized Green's trademark phrase. By then, of course, Red Or Dead

was one of the UK's leading fashion brands, going on to win the British Fashion Council's 'Street Style Designer of the Year' award three times in a row. After 21 consecutive seasons on the catwalk at the London Fashion Week, Wayne and Gerardine sold Red Or Dead in a multimillion-pound cash sale.

'We fell into Red Or Dead with no money and fell out with lots; but most of all it was a challenge and fantastic fun from beginning to end.' Since then, the Hemingways have designed carpets, wall coverings, menswear ranges for retail outlets and even a mass-market, 700-unit housing project for Wimpey in Tyneside.

RED OR DEAD

Red or Dead

Michelle Banarse

"Who would have thought over 40 years ago a boot such as the 1460 would have such an impact on fashion, subculture and music. It was a great honour to be able to leave my mark on one of the most iconic British items of the last four decades."

> "Our worst fear is not that we are inadequate. Our deepest fear is that we are powerful."

Nelson Mandela

charged concerts – the Artists Against Apartheid 'Freedom Beat' on London's Clapham Common in 1986 and, most famously of all, 1988's Nelson Mandela Concert at Wembley Stadium for the imprisoned anti-apartheid campaigner's 70th birthday. Eighteen months later, Mandela was set free.

SHARP (Skinheads Against Racial Prejudice) is just one of several skinhead organizations that fight prejudice and racism. In Germany, in particular, there has been some overt activity by fascists, and even racist-motivated murders, which has brought about a groundswell of anti-fascist sentiment in that country. Of the estimated 8,000 skinheads in Germany, over 20 per cent are believed to be adherents of SHARP.

Inevitably, such close associations with skins have generated acres of bad publicity for Dr. Martens. For a boot that was designed to alleviate pain, it is ironic that it first came to public prominence for inflicting hurt. The toecap, the thick sole, the supportive lower legs – all elements that make DM's a healthy choice – have at times been hijacked entirely by the more violent sections of society. Some observers dubbed the boot 'a boxing glove for the feet', and tabloid pictures of old ladies with Dr. Martens footprints on their faces did little to assuage public concern.

Klaus Maertens, who died in 1988, would have been horrified to see his medical invention used in such a way. At one point, AirWair was phoned up by one tabloid newspaper editor demanding to know why the company continued to make boots that precipitated such violence. In response, Max Griggs said, 'It's not the boot that kicks heads in, it's the people who wear them. You can be violent in anything.' As a notable aside, it is worth mentioning that adherents of extreme right-wing groups tend to wear army boots with toecaps, rather than DM's.

Global appeal

Since the '50s, Britain's youth culture has proved to be one of the country's most consistent and popular exports. Although the teddy boy remained essentially an English phenomenon, since its invention generations of subcultural styles and music have crossed the globe; in the process, inevitably mutating into new hybrids, and generating a constant shredding and recycling of ideas.

Such international appeal has meant that Dr. Martens have been perhaps Britain's most significant contribution to global anti-fashion and counter-culture over the last 40 years. More importantly, the boot's iconic status has been created by the marketplace, not sold to it. What makes this situation even more remarkable is the fact that, up until the '80s, there was only a handful of styles available. Furthermore, prior to the '80s the boots' limited export availability meant that DM's could only trickle abroad.

All that changed in 1988. This year saw several notable events. George Bush followed two-term Ronald Reagan into the White House, and – perhaps no coincidence – the drug Prozac

Right: Anti-Nazi League logo.

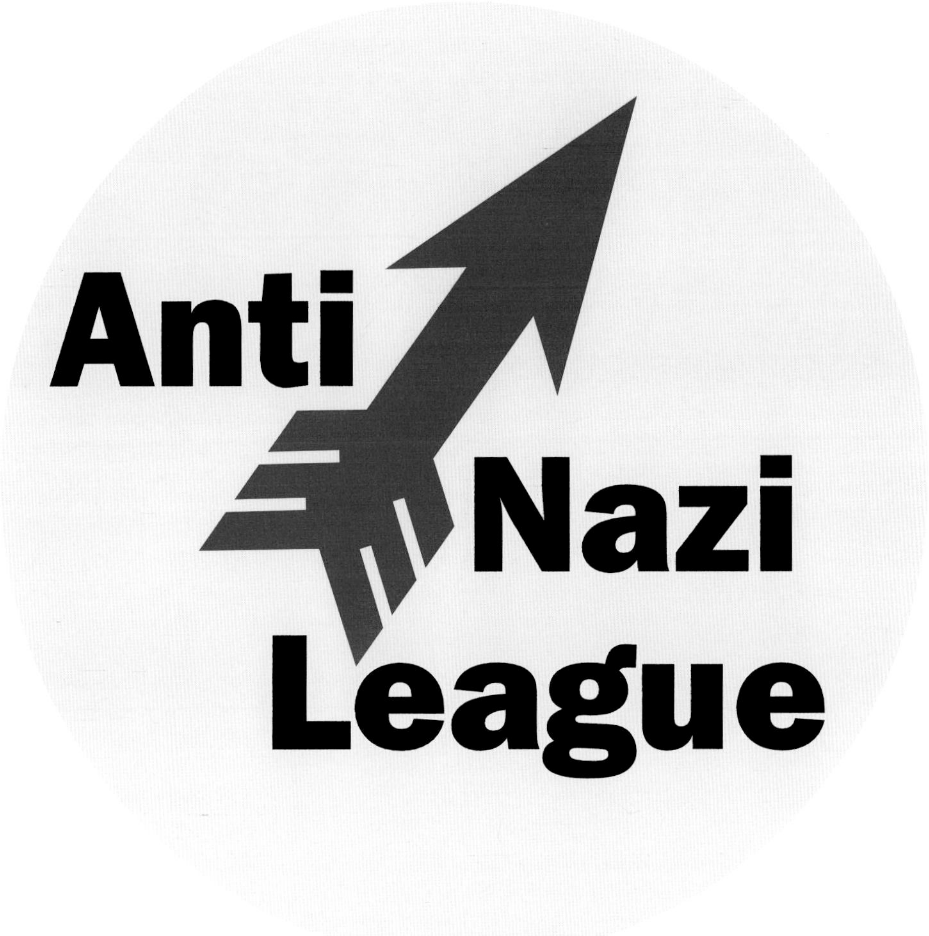
Anti
Nazi
League

Dr. Martens AirWair with Bouncing Soles

EXPORT QUALITY

MADE IN ENGLAND

"Fashion is a form of ugliness so intolerable that we have to alter it every six months."

Oscar Wilde

was launched. It was also an important date for Dr. Martens – not because any new style was launched, nor because a new subculture had latched onto the boot, but simply because of a supposedly mundane administrative happening: AirWair Ltd's 'Export Quality' was created.

In America, the boot's restricted availability prior to this meant that DM's were hard to track down (although, in some senses, this gave some added kudos to the brand). The influx began in California, before spreading via word of mouth and among various subcultures to other cities.

By 1993, the boot was grabbing headlines across the US for trouncing the trainer market that had for so long been dominant. Surfers, skateboarders, punks, grunge kids, metal heads and industrial fans were just a few of the subcultures who picked up on Dr. Martens.

Left: Advertising DM's abroad.

As in Britain, the boot has had its darker moments, mainly due to its associations with neo-fascism. Some US schools banned Docs from uniform lists because of what were seen as unsavoury connotations; one school in Grapevine, Texas, experienced a pupil walkout in protest after the decision to ban the boot from school premises. Generally, however, Doc Martens have proved very popular in the United States, providing a rare beacon of UK culture in America after several decades of postwar Americanization of Great Britain.

In the Far East, the boot found a niche that quickly blossomed into a major phenomenon. China had for a long time suppressed the rise of rock music; indeed, the authorities once denounced rock and roll as 'pornographic', consequently banning it. (A pamphlet was issued with the title 'How to Recognize Pornographic Music'; it even listed jazz.) However, such oppression could not halt the growing interest in Western

culture, and its impact in terms of music created an indigenous subculture in China. More recently, the party line was (albeit reluctantly) changed, and limited scope was created for the modern music, with an official statement announcing that, in certain cases, it could be seen as 'healthy exercise for young and old'.

Over in Hong Kong, matters were somewhat more liberal. Docs had filtered through in tiny quantities before 1990, but once the export floodgates were opened, that island's thirst for all things British meant that the boots became a massive hit. The early months of 1994 saw a phase of bell-bottoms worn with 1460s; elsewhere, the twenty-eyelet boots have proved very popular. Demand has become so great in certain areas that a thriving second-hand market has developed, with a few rare styles selling for more than new boots. Similar cult status has been afforded in Japan, where English influences have combined with the youngsters' own unique styles to see the boot used in a myriad of ways.

As with America, Australasia's affair with Doc Martens was boosted by the arrival of grunge. In Germany, the sole's original homeland, some 100,000 pairs

"The sickening politics that are involved with being a successful commercial rock band are real aggravating. No one has any idea."

Kurt Cobain

had been sold back by 1993. There were tales of empty container lorries from the Eastern Bloc and Russia drawing up outside the Wollaston factory with orders for hundreds of pairs to take back home. Even in France, a nation traditionally somewhat averse to British culture, the boot found its own corner of the market. It was now a truly global icon.

Status symbol

The '80s managed, somehow, to close on a note of triumph, despite a legacy of upheaval and, occasionally, catastrophe; millions of previously oppressed people now enjoyed levels of freedom and democracy that would have been unthinkable only a few years beforehand.

The staggering advances in computer technology had turned the world of work on its head – especially in the media, where the quickening pace was only just beginning to hint at the technological leaps that would characterize the '90s.

It had been an unforgettable decade for Dr. Martens, too. Remarkably, despite the rise of the sneaker, the proliferation of ever-more bewildering and fragmented subcultural groups, plus the general trend away from such simple and utilitarian items, Dr. Martens waved goodbye to the '80s in a far healthier state than that in which it had entered those years. Its iconic status now assured, the boot seemed to have risen above fleeting fashion trends, and to have established sales figures that only a select few footwear companies could dream. With 30 years of success and year-on-year sales growth that showed no sign of slowing, Dr. Martens entered the '90s with more 'reasons to be cheerful' than ever before.

Right: Japanese youth culture often adopts exaggerated versions of western street style.

It started with grunge and ended with its direct descendant, nu-metal. Yet the '90s were much more than just a paean to the electric guitar. 'Cool Britannia' came and went, pop made a comeback and, somehow, throughout it all Dr. Martens maintained a following, with a niche in most corners of youth subculture.

90s

1960-1990

Dr. Martens

AirWair

WITH Bouncing SOLES

LIMITED · EDITION

'90s

The world in 1990 was a very different place for the millions of people who had so recently been freed from the misery of living behind the Iron Curtain. With the collapse of the Eastern Bloc, Europe was experiencing a new dawn – Germany was reunified, and there were free elections in Romania.

However, ethnic in-fighting and violence soon raised their ugly heads, as former countries splintered into rival factions and bloody conflicts raged across the face of Europe, with ethnic cleansing being witnessed on a scale not seen since the Nazis.

Liberation was not just confined to Europe. In a remarkable turn of events over in South Africa, Nelson Mandela emerged from three decades behind bars to take power as president of that previously apartheid-riven country. In the Middle East, the Gulf War aimed – superficially at least – to liberate Kuwait from the invading Iraqi forces. However, the repercussions of Middle-Eastern politics and questions about the world's oil supply were sufficiently complex, a decade on, to bring a post-9/11 world to the brink of conflict once more. (Chillingly, on 26 February 1993, an explosion at the World Trade Center in New York killed five people in a foretaste of events.)

The human race's taste for self-destruction contrasted with science's growing prowess for prolonging life expectancy. The beginnings of gene therapy may have hinted to some that Aldous Huxley's 'brave new world' was lurking just around the corner, but the research sped along, punctuated by astonishing breakthroughs. Such advances – which included eliminating polio and tuberculosis – were tempered by an upsurge in deaths from cancer and the still-festering blight of Aids, particularly in Africa. Nonetheless, the sense of standing on the threshold of a new era was reinforced by Bill Clinton's defeat of George Bush Senior in 1992, as the United States tried to haul itself out of a recession that had infected both itself and much of the Western world. Japan was surging ahead as a new economic superpower, but would reach the end of the decade in financial disarray and deep recession.

Meanwhile, the acquittals of four white LAPD officers in the Rodney King trial saw Los Angeles erupt in rioting, a clear reminder that in this liberal, free-thinking world, racism was still a wide flesh wound in

Right: (clockwise from top left)
Nelson Mandela; the ozone hole photographed by a satellite; the HIV virus; US soldiers in the first Gulf War.

ANTARCTIC OZONE HOLE

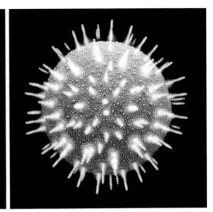

> "Women have been ingratiating themselves to men for too long. If you want to be nice to men, then there are plenty of ways of doing so that don't involve wearing ridiculous shoes on your feet."

Dr Halla Beloff, social psychologist at Edinburgh University

America's side. Conversely, the world marvelled as O.J. Simpson was acquitted of the murder of his wife and her lover in a television trial that broke all viewing records.

Fresh winds were blowing across the UK, too. Britain was starting to crack in its second decade of Conservative rule. Thatcher had revolutionized the nation with radical and rampant privatization, gutted the welfare state and all but demolished the unions. However, her ill-judged imposition of the poll tax was the start of her downfall, and it prompted countrywide condemnation and rioting in central London. The 'Iron Lady's' popularity plunged.

Just one year into the '90s, Thatcher was replaced by the

Left: Noel Gallagher of Oasis.

'grey' but affable John Major – a man who had, by way of numerous Machiavellian manoeuvres, made the journey from 16-year-old dole-queue regular to someone capable of replacing one of Britain's most feared politicians. However, the post-Thatcher years brought Major's 'Back to Basics' campaign – during which time, it transpired much later, Major was actually conducting an extra-marital affair – and a crumbling economy, which added fuel to the calls of 'It's Time For A Change'.

New Labour, fronted by the Cheshire Cat of the Commons, Tony Blair, promised a fresh start. The party swept to victory in the landslide election of 1997. At first, this prompted the coining of the phrase 'Cool Britannia', with British bands,

fashions, culture and films enjoying renewed popularity around the world, in a throwback to the heady days of the '60s.

Golden years

The '90s were a decade in which the shoe industry exploded and became commercially colossal. Brands no longer manufactured one particular style or group of styles. Shoes were becoming available in every possible colour, material, design and construction. The sneaker was more of a fashion statement than a fitness necessity. Thankfully, the revival of older shoes, such as the Clarks desert boot, plus the re-emergence of the platform boot (fuelled by Spice Girls mania, which largely bypassed Dr. Martens) and the 1460, acted as a counterbalance to the array of products. At times, these looked more like science fiction than footwear fact. Shoes were now advertised as a lifestyle product, not just something you put on your feet, with celebrity endorsements and high-profile ad campaigns emphasizing everyone's idealistic feel-good and look-even-better potential.

Despite this fierce competition, the '90s were golden years for Dr. Martens, as several underground movements

> "If anyone gives you criticism that starts off 'You should' or 'You shouldn't', walk away immediately."

Paul Westerberg of The Replacements, 1995

and new groups of wearers emerged. One welcome addition to the DM's' family was the exorbitant increase in female buyers. This trend began to evolve during the mid to late '80s, particularly with the more colourful designs of Wayne Hemingway and the subsequent factory-produced styles.

By the middle of the '90s, female Dr. Martens wearers accounted for 50 per cent of total sales, a figure that would have been incomprehensible back in the '60s during the brand's workwear genesis. However, things had changed somewhat since the launch of the first Dr. Martens boot. Although women had been wearing DM's for years, generally they were seen on female punks or skins, who preferred the 1460 or the shoe (but only if they could find a size that was small enough!). However, in the mid '80s, all that started to change.

More than ever, women were dressing for themselves, not for men, and the resulting melange of styles and ideas saw seemingly inappropriate items being thrown together in new combinations. Thus it was that the classic style of a flowery dress with a big pair of clumpy Docs found its way into many girls' wardrobes. The boots tempered the overt femininity of the pretty dresses, and at the same time reduced any inherent vulnerability that such flimsy garments might convey. Sociologists hailed the new trend as an emancipation of sorts, while many ardent feminists championed the boot and shoe as a symbol of female assertiveness. Such 'proletarian chic', as some observers called it, was a definite rebellion against more traditional women's clothing. For other women, though, it was simply a great relief to be wearing a comfortable pair of shoes.

Throughout much of history, women's footwear has been far from practical. Chinese foot-binding was an extreme example, and for centuries it was used to manacle women to men. In seventeenth-century Europe, husbands insisted that their wives wear heeled shoes, making it virtually impossible for them to walk on the cobbled streets outside. This vision of the ideal woman as a weak and sedentary creature who lived almost entirely indoors was still in vogue some two hundred years later. Indeed, when the flat-soled, weatherproof boot was introduced for women in the 1830s, there was outrage among the less liberal sectors of male society, who were horrified by these newly mobile women. In France, centuries previously, one of the charges brought against Joan of Arc had been that she dressed in men's boots, 'up to her thighs'.

For the modern woman, the stiletto was similarly debilitating. Aside from the sexual connotations of the shoe, it was never suited to walking, nor did it offer any degree of security in the event of a difficult situation necessitating a quick escape. Many feminists saw the stiletto as the natural successor to Chinese foot-binding.   ↓

Right: An advertisement for DM's shows that the female wearer is now a force – from an early age.

YOU TELL HER SHE CAN'T WEAR THEM

Kids just know what they want.

Dave & Joe
(David Kappo and Joe Bates)

"We wore Docs in school and we wanted the boots to reflect that teenage rebelliousness of customizing the standard into the unique, in the same way that we used to mess around with our school uniforms."

Indeed, in the same summer as DM's' original launch, Dr W. Bamber wrote in *Shoe & Leather News*: '[Society should] ban all stiletto heels – how women can balance in them I don't know . . . The answer is to encourage girls to wear sensible shoes, but I am afraid the dictates of fashion might prevail.'

From their inception, in addition to their comfort factor, a pair of Docs also accentuated the foot and looked strong and well constructed, conveying an impression of power and feminine independence.

By the start of the '90s, millions of women worldwide owned more than one pair of Dr. Martens. The burgeoning women's market led to a flurry of fantastic Dr. Martens styles, colours and patterns; many of them were based initially on a variant of the 1460. Thousands of female fans even walked down the aisle in white patent-leather pairs – DM's spotted this trend and started to manufacture a gold pair covered with white lace (as worn by this writer's wife on her wedding day).

Such extravagance was not new, however. In the 1890s, 'opera boots' were hand-painted

Left: Flowered-patterned Docs; these were now one of many vibrant designs.

The author's wife, Kaye, sporting her gold Docs on their wedding day.

with detailed flowers and proved very popular in English high society. The rising demand for girls' DM's eventually led to more innovative styles such as high-heeled DM's, which were introduced in autumn 1993 (and tested by Stephen Griggs' own postmistress, Mary Barnes) and even platform soles, called Quads. Designers hooked on to the idea, anchoring the frail look of many of their more

Also in 1990

- McDonalds opens its first restaurant in Moscow.

- The Gulf War breaks out after Iraq invades Kuwait.

- It took radio over 40 years to reach a global audience of 50 million; it took television 15 years to do the same. The Internet achieved that in less than 36 months.

Also in 1991

- Yugoslavia falls apart and the Soviet Union disintegrates as parliaments in various Soviet republics declare their independence.

- Moviegoers are astounded by computer special effects in *Terminator 2*.

- *The Silence of the Lambs* starring Anthony Hopkins and Jodie Foster terrifies audiences.

- Data transmission through optical fibres is launched; the process can work at 32 billion bits per second.

- An X-ray photo is taken of the effort the brain makes in recalling a word.

outlandish catwalk creations with a solid pair of Docs.

One of the most entertaining aspects of this development was the absolute horror and consternation created by girls wearing Docs. Vast sections of society seemed to lose faith in human nature, and hastily predicted the downfall of Generation X. Parents were appalled to see their beautiful daughters wearing the same boots as a skinhead. The media also had many doubters. Take this comment from a clearly unimpressed Mike Lockley of the *Rugeley Post*: 'Do today's young women honestly believe Doc Martens boots go with dresses? Or [that] they look more alluring with studs in their noses?'

Fortunately, the look was so popular that it even filtered into modern works of fiction, including this extract from Jane Owen's novel, *Camden Girls*: 'Just look at the way women walk in a pair of Doc Martens . . . Bold, confident and mobile. No more teetering about like Bambi on acid.'

It is somewhat ironic that the workwear boot that first came to notoriety for its macho image is now regarded by many as the quintessential unisex footwear. It is fair to say that Doc Martens have revolutionized shoe fashion

for women – a 16-year-old girl is now far more likely to buy a pair of DM's as her first solo purchase than a traditional women's shoe or a towering pair of stilettos.

Grunge chic

At the start of the decade, a new cultural phenomenon spread across the globe and revolutionized the world of music and youth fashion. Its epicentre was the far north-western seaboard of the US, in Seattle, Washington. Prior to the '90s, Seattle was not famed for its alternative music. Of course, it could claim Jimi Hendrix among its forefathers, and there were other successes, such as the Sonics, the Fleetwoods, and several more mainstream artists including Robert Cray, Heart, Kenny G, Quincy Jones and Queensryche. Yet these successes were sporadic and isolated, with no thread of association between the respective artists.

However, as the '80s hurtled towards their climax, an underground scene was developing that, during a brief flurry of breathtaking musical brilliance, would turn the global mainstream on its head. Grunge's backdrop was the sweeping recession that was

"Nineties style isn't."

David Borenstein, December 1999

suffocating the economies of the Western world in the early '90s. America suffered as much as any country, and with predictable social results – alienation, poverty and rebellion.

Although grunge was absolutely a US-born movement, it found thousands of welcoming fans in the UK, where the recession was resulting in similarly disenchanted millions. Countless homeowners were still deep in negative equity, thanks to the collapse of the housing market in the late '80s. Unemployment queues were lengthy and dissatisfaction with Tory rule growing. The student population was boiling with anger at the introduction of university fees, sweeping reforms of the National Health Service and other national 'institutions'. All this and more made the UK and other countries in Europe a hotbed of discontent and pessimism – characteristics into which grunge tapped directly.

Starting in that cold, north-western corner of the United States, grunge began life as a

Right: Stage-diving into a festival mosh pit.

"Grunge is what happens when children of divorce get their hands on guitars."

Newsweek

disparate group of bands gigging relentlessly on the underground circuit, with no real eye for the ensuing avalanche of multi-platinum record sales and sold-out world tours. The record label Sub Pop is seen by many people as having been at the very heart of this era of music. Released under it was a seminal series of limited-edition records and classic tracks by bands such as Sonic Youth, Steve Fisk, the U-Men, Skinny Puppy, Nirvana and the often-overlooked Green River.

In addition to these names, there were hordes of other bands producing alternative music of note at this period. The quite brilliant Tad, Mudhoney, the Screaming Trees – these and many others released music that, to the youth of the day at least, was revolutionary. Established bands like the Melvins and Sonic Youth also enjoyed rejuvenated careers in the wake of numerous citations

Left: Nirvana.

from the younger bands they had influenced.

Older detractors derided grunge's fusion of hardcore and metal as merely rehashing '70s rock, but this mattered little to those who were experiencing such music for the first time. It felt to them like they were living through something important. Besides, the scuzzy, furious raw energy of grunge was rooted much more in the post-punk barrage of US hardcore bands such as Black Flag, who themselves were compared to bands such as Led Zeppelin. Also, there was a clear lineage back to '60s garage bands like the Sonics, MC5, the Stooges and the Kingsmen.

Like so many underground musical movements, this latest development was only tagged after it had already been around for some time (indeed, the label 'grunge' was itself originally a tongue-in-cheek tag). By then Nirvana had gone global with their ten-million-selling *Nevermind* album, which ↓

Also in 1992

- By this year, 65 million personal computers had been sold.

- After a televised State-of-the-Nation speech by President Bush, 25 million viewers phone in with their opinions.

- Bill Clinton claims victory in the US elections, ending the Reagan–Bush Republican era.

- Cable TV mogul John Malone is greeted with scorn by many when he predicts that there may be as many as 500 channels in the near future.

Also in 1993

- Frank Zappa and River Phoenix die.

- The blockbuster movies *Jurassic Park* and *Schindler's List* are released.

- Despite rumours that mobile phones or cellphones cause brain cancer, sales rise exponentially.

- The first text messages are sent between Nokia mobile/cellphones.

- Digital cameras are introduced.

Amanda Wakely

"I wanted to play on the fact that Dr. Martens are the ultimate utility boot by turning them into the ultimate 'glamour' boot, using strong colour and a fur trim . . . Utility and luxury all in one!"

"If music be the food of love, let's have a bite of your maracas."

Graffiti in New York, 1991

single-handedly changed the face of modern music programming, live shows, record-store buying policies and just about every facet of the music and entertainment industries. For example, in the wake of 'Smells Like Teen Spirit', MTV's aesthetic was transformed virtually overnight, ditching the bikini-clad babes of a thousand soft-porn metal videos and replacing them with grunge's grittier, cheaper look. For the next two years, grunge ruled the world.

With the music came the culture – grunge, like punk before it, was truly thrift-store chic. Bedecked in flannel shirts, oversized shorts cut off just below the knee and sporting long, lank locks, the grunge kid quickly picked up the tag of 'loser'. Girls often wore flowery dresses with thick leggings, or trousers with oversized band T-shirts. And on the feet of both the male and female grunge kids were, invariably, a pair of DM's. These were usually black, and more often than not the 1460 (despite the recent rash of more

flamboyant designs). Laces were frequently coloured and left untied, so that the sides of the quarter flapped loosely around the ankles. Occasionally, band logos were painted on the boot, although generally the look was very simple and unfettered by decoration. This was dressing-down at its farthest extreme – the boot's status as an 'anti-label' fitted in perfectly with the anti-establishment feeling. Converse also enjoyed a renewal of popularity at this time.

After the close of the '80s, when sales of Dr. Martens had fallen, this adoption of the boot by grunge reopened the floodgates for Docs, sending them in vast quantities for the first time into Australasia, the US, Japan and many other territories. After a lengthy phase during which trainers had ruled the footwear world, it was a welcome return.

Unfortunately, as with so many subcultures, once grunge had entered the mainstream it was rendered culturally impotent, in effect castrated by its own success. Nirvana's debut album

was produced for just $606.17; later, cheque-book-waving A&R men would be jetting into Seattle and throwing six-figure sums at just about any band. Some of these gambles paid off with multimillion-selling albums; but many bands never fulfilled their early promise, unprepared as they were for the intense heat of the worldwide spotlight.

Million-dollar marketing campaigns backed all the latest 'grungers', while cheesy TV shows ran features on what to say to your 'loser' teenager. Elevator music albums were released with muzak versions of grunge classics and, perhaps worst of all, haute couture designers began to copy the style.

Milan and Paris catwalks exhibited horrendous copies of the grunge look, with obscenely priced and hideously shaped versions of the thrift-store style. Record stores reported fashion journalists, dripping in designer accessories, running in and asking for albums by grunge bands. Some even tried to re-title the designer wear 'frunge'. Lumberjack shirts with designer names were now selling for over $500 and a corduroy jacket, similar to the thousands of second-hand coats

Right: Grunge fashion hits the catwalk.

> "In the twelfth century, if musicians didn't play in front of the king correctly, we would have been beheaded. We were minstrels and fools. Now we're icons and deities and demi-gods."

Al Jourgenson of Ministry, 1993

worn by grunge fans, was offered for sale for $3,000.

And then, of course, it all stopped. The shot that was heard across the world when Kurt Cobain committed suicide in early April 1994 effectively put an end to grunge – although, for many, it had already been stymied by the corporate hijack, the growing drug problems and the increasingly feeble music. In the vacuum left by Cobain's death, the grunge movement splintered, stumbled and ultimately self-imploded.

Fortunately, in America bands like Green Day and Offspring filled the void with their post-punk energy. They were met with multimillion sales, as there still seemed to be a thirst for the punk ethos. These bands

Left: Post-punk rockers, Green Day.

enjoyed high-profile commercial success, and they appeared to take the snarling punk beast right into the very heart of corporate America.

By contrast, there were also Doc-wearing bands, such as Rancid, which took a somewhat more eclectic approach. Rancid are one of America's most compelling bands. Mixing Two Tone ska with Clash-influenced punk, covering Oi! band The Blitz and working with members of The Specials, they are indeed a strange mix. Their eponymous debut album heralded a run of independently released albums that put the fire back into a rapidly ailing MTV American-rock circuit.

Their second album was recorded and mixed in just four days. The third long player, *And Out Come The Wolves*, sold over

Also in 1994

- The Channel Tunnel – the 'Chunnel' – opens, having cost $15 billion to build.

- Writer Charles Bukowski and Nirvana frontman Kurt Cobain die.

- Los Angeles is rocked by a severe earthquake.

- Pizza Hut starts taking customers' orders over the Web.

- Country music is confirmed as US radio's most popular musical format.

- Yahoo! Internet search engine is started by two Stanford engineering graduates – four years later, it will be worth $70 billion.

Also in 1995

- A nerve-gas attack on the Tokyo underground system strikes terror into the heart of every urban commuter worldwide.

- The deadly flesh-eating Ebola virus gains notoriety.

- *Toy Story* becomes the first totally digital feature-length film.

- In Cleveland, Ohio, the Rock and Roll Hall of Fame Museum opens.

"One-fifth of the people are against everything all the time."

Al Jourgenson of Ministry, 1993

half a million copies and featured more of the lightning-fast brevity, snarling lyrics and razor-sharp guitars that made their live shows such a riot. With their 1998 album, *Life Won't Wait*, Rancid found themselves one of the biggest alternative bands on the planet. When offered $1.5 million to sign to Epic Records, they declined, choosing instead to remain with their independent record company, Epitaph. The reason? 'We're friends with just about everybody on the label.'

Industrial rock

The mid '90s also saw a second scene emerge from the US, which again championed the Dr. Martens boot. The hugely commercial progeny of the aforementioned goth scene came with the explosion of so-called 'industrial' music early in the '90s. Most visibly prevalent in America, this scene centred on bands such as Ministry, My Life With The Thrill Kill Kult, Skinny Puppy, Front 242 and Revolting Cocks, with the most famous act being Trent Reznor's Nine Inch

Nails. In the UK, acts such as Sheep On Drugs and Nitzer Ebb flew the crunching industrial flag. Largely a scene of media invention (as indeed many are), none of these bands aspired to or acknowledged the industrial title, but there were, all the same, certain musical features giving them a common thread, albeit a loose one.

The sonic backdrop to most industrial music is an extreme electronic soundscape. Fearfully hard metallic guitars are mixed with throbbing sample-heavy and often-repetitious keyboards, maniacal vocals, frequently delivered through a distorted megaphone, and a thunderous and repetitious double-bass beat. Lyrically, the degree of cynicism, bitterness, loathing and hatred was acute, scathingly detailing themes of alienation, social exclusion, pain, depression, oppression and control. Ironically, this nihilistic sound and stance was often highly danceable, a fact that enabled industrial to establish a fast, fierce grip on the more festering corners of the

underground club scene.

Shredded black clothing and leather garb adorned the bands and fans, as did multiple body piercing, while a generally apocalyptic tone to their gigs set a morbid and fascinating new movement in motion. Violent moshing was taken to new extremes at many of these gigs, and the stage shows often resembled something straight out of some cult sci-fi B movie.

Many saw industrial as responding to the clarion call of rebellious rhetoric that punk had failed to sustain – indeed, a specific similarity could be found in the popularity of slam dancing in industrial clubs. However, the beast of industrial rock was a mutated blend of numerous antecedents, not just punk. Tracing the movement's origins right back to its inception necessarily invokes acts such as Can from Germany, whose first album, *Monster Music*, is considered an industrial classic.

In the early '70s, Kraftwerk had used only electronic instruments and devices for their entirely synthetic music, an idea that was highly innovative at the time. For many, this band was the single most important

Right: Fans of industrial music cited the energy of the scene's raucous gigs.

industrial group ever. Later in the '70s and during the '80s, the post-punk experimentalism of acts such as Throbbing Gristle were often cited as seminal.

Throbbing Gristle were a half-punk, half-performance art group that rehearsed in the 'Death Factory', which was rumored to be adjacent to what had been a mass grave for bubonic plague victims in the seventeenth century. As well as laying many of the foundations for industrial music, Throbbing Gristle – or 'TG', as they were dubbed – also launched the trend for military or pseudo-political adornments on their clothing, with dark T-shirts emblazoned with embroidered patches, badges and stark logos. This was often matched with invented institutional names, such as 'The Ministry of Antisocial Insecurity'.

Seen as the forefathers of industrial, TG in turn revered the work of US West Coast artist Monte Cazazza, who is said to have invented the term industrial – Throbbing Gristle's record label was also called Industrial. Others claimed that writer William S. Burroughs' 'cut-and-paste' audio

Left: Genesis P. Orridge of industrial band Throbbing Gristle.

experiments in the '60s and the work of other Beat writers had cast the first seed.

There were also early bands such as Wire, SPK, Leather Nun and, most notoriously, Einsturzende Neubaten, who famously created music without instruments, opting instead for the melodic capabilities of hammers, metalworking and factory implements. One source has suggested that the lead singer Blixa once wired his chest up to a microphone and then had someone crack his ribs, just to capture that unique sound. The use of such unorthodox sounds expanded in the '90s to include a wider spectrum of samples, such as machine-gun fire or referential clips from obscure movies or TV clips, giving rise to a new incarnation of industrial.

Industrial music bubbled underground – with the occasional visitation to the mainstream – for many years, splicing through the work of acts such as Cabaret Voltaire and even Depeche Mode. However, it wasn't until the early '90s and the global popularity of bands such as Nine Inch Nails that the music saw its first chart-topping successes. Of course, by then the original tenets of industrial had changed

Also in 1996

- Madonna finally wins critical acclaim for her performance in a film, albeit a musical, *Evita*.

- The flat-panel computer monitor is introduced.

- The US Postal Service processes 600 million items of mail per day.

- Use of e-mail is beginning to take over office communications – the world of media and broadcasting is similarly transformed. The publishing giant Associated Press once had 1,500 telegraph operators, now it has four.

Also in 1997

- Elton John's 'Candle in the Wind '97', written to celebrate the life of the late Diana, Princess of Wales, sells 32 million copies in 37 days.

- An IBM computer defeats world chess champion Garry Kasparov.

- *Titanic* becomes the biggest-grossing film of all time, costing $300 million to make, but grossing double that.

"I wore Doc Martens as well and looked dead cool."

Noel Gallagher of Oasis suffered from a kidney infection as a child and was allowed to wear long trousers to school

enormously; the music, clothing and motivation of such acts were also markedly different from their forebears.

At the start of the '90s, certain industrial acts began to shift phenomenal quantities of records and to pack out concert halls around the world – clearly, there was something about their approach that was tapping into the music-listening public's psyche. The exaggerated rage appealed to millions, drawing them into industrial's dark hyper-reality and self-loathing. It was music that reflected a time when serial killers had become little more than interesting bar gossip, and where sex and death were intertwined – it was a feral, sporadic and nihilistic sound, straddling the worlds of punk, dance, metal and grunge.

Nine Inch Nails were always – albeit reluctantly – at the more commercial tip of this movement, although mainman Reznor always refused to categorize his music so simplistically. For example,

some said that NIN's debut long player, *Pretty Hate Machine*, had been the first million-selling industrial album. The record label at the epicentre of this movement was America's Wax Trax; yet some of the biggest-selling industrial records were 'hijacked' by major labels keen to own a slice of this latest phenomenon.

This early-to-mid '90s scene had many of the original elements of older goth – the fishnets, the black-and-white make-up (for both men and women), and the jet-black hair – although the music was much heavier. During 1994, when industrial music was at its commercial zenith, millions of kids the world over donned black clothes and corresponding DM's. Black eight-holers were the staple item, although a few more ardent goth sartorialists would venture out in a pair with sixteen eyelets or more.

Occasionally, both the fashion and the music of industrial would edge onto the fringes of the fetish scene, with the use of

leather, rubber and PVC often cropping up in both spheres – again, usually anchored by a pair of classic 1460s.

Britpop

Back in Britain, the US domination of the music scene had been boring many people for many months, if not years. Inevitably, music that provided a stark contrast to the dour miserabilism of much of grunge and industrial began to emerge. It would eventually lead to one of British music's most fertile periods: Britpop.

The tail end of the '80s had seen two great British music scenes, neither of which had much interest in Dr. Martens. The rave scene, which originated within the circle of the M25 motorway and centred, initially at least, in Essex, found no place in its all-night dance marathons for the heavy 1460. Although occasionally seen on the feet of dancing ravers, the boots were not the footwear of choice (trainers tended to rule the day). However, the illicit nature of these massive raves, plus the cutting-edge music, the pirate-radio transmissions and establishment disapproval,

Right: From girl-power to patent power; the Doc dipped into the fetish domain.

> "Shoes excite me. Lager excites me. America excites me. Stools excite me. Everything excites me. I'm just one excited young man."

Liam Gallagher

meant that many people from other subcultures soon became caught up in the scene, and they did indeed wear DM's away from the raves themselves.

The last great British musical statement of the '80s had been in the spring of 1989, with the so-called 'Madchester' scene – the Mancunian corner of the music world once again providing a plethora of bands to revolutionize the rock and dance format. The Stone Roses led the way, with The Happy Mondays and Inspiral Carpets following closely behind, as 'baggy' music swept the nation up in a tide of flares, long-sleeved shirts and Joe Bloggs clothing. There was no place in this fashion for eight-eyelet boots, only brand-name trainers. Also, these bands struggled to export their culture across the Atlantic to America, a problem that many

Left: The rave scene brings an entirely new dimension to the UK's dance scene.

British groups endured over the next ten years, as the US found little of interest in the various English genres that sprang up.

Britpop was the next great British musical scene. The first whiffs of this new movement came in 1993 with the early singles of a band called Suede, led by the enigmatic and inspirational Brett Anderson. Set against the backdrop of slacker-driven grunge culture outlined earlier in this chapter, Suede's songs spoke of stylized and romantic London dramas, and Brett's peculiarly camp Englishness carried it all off to perfection. Suede had swagger, style and above all the songs – they were heralded famously by *Melody Maker* with the front-page headline, 'The Best New Band in Britain'. They did indeed change the face of British music – it was a million miles away from grunge's by-now tiresome machismo and mainstream corporate feel.

Also in 1998

- *Harry Potter and the Sorcerer's Stone*, the first of the J.K. Rowling series, hits book stores and single-handedly rewrites every book-selling record. The tale of witchery gets the whole globe reading again (as well as making spectacles fashionable for children for the first time).

- America announces that it has 50,000 publishers.

- A Web site, called 'The Drudge Report', breaks news of the scandalous Clinton–Lewinsky affair.

Also in 1999

- A $35,000 movie, *The Blair Witch Project*, becomes a blockbuster and forces the multimillion-dollar movie industry to rethink its approach.

- Computer viruses are virulent and frequent, leading to newly defined criminal offences.

- The Y2K (Year 2000) causes panic globally, yet very little tangible disruption ensues.

- The Ikonos satellite is able to detect an object on Earth as small as a card table.

> "People say that everything's been said. How defeatist is that? Art is an expression of humanity and, just because people have been saying the same things for two thousand years, doesn't rob those things of their potency. You can't just give up on it. There's always different ways of saying the same things."

Brett Anderson, Suede

The explosion of Britpop was pre-empted by a clumsily titled scene called the New Wave of New Wave. This was populated by trainer- or Doc-Martens-wearing, speed-snorting energetic bands who were as important sartorially as they were musically – SMASH, Elastica and These Animal Men worshipped bands like The Clash and The Sex Pistols, but enjoyed only fleeting success as the approaching juggernaut of Britpop pushed them aside.

Britpop really started to blossom in 1993, boosted by Blur's pivotal second album, *Modern Life Is Rubbish*, which openly paraded the band's Anglo-centric interests. With the recession fading and, with it, the sense of gloom that had made grunge seem so appropriate in the UK, the kids on the block began to look for something more uplifting. The much-anticipated arrival of Suede's eponymous debut album signalled another step away from the spiralling self-destructive tendencies of grunge-by-numbers. The festivals that bands like Nirvana and Pearl Jam had revitalized were now taken over by a string of newly confident British bands – Blur, Suede, The Boo Radleys,

Pulp and even a rejuvenated New Order.

The untimely death of Kurt Cobain and the arrival of Blur's third album, *Parklife*, sparked the deluge. Suddenly, there was a wash of superb British bands, with quirky albums and massive followings. British youth abruptly put their grunge clothing away and started rifling through records by British bands again. Cut-off shorts and plaid shirts were returned to the charity stores, and long hair was cut short. In came a variant of the early '80s casual look, mixed with elements of mod and other unique styles, including the odd Hawaiian shirt! Trainers were popular, Harrington jackets made another comeback and even the Oxfam look of Pulp's Jarvis Cocker was copied by many Britpop fans.

Once again, Dr. Martens managed to be accepted by this new generation of music aficionados. Many of the Britpop bands had listened to the likes of The Clash, Buzzcocks, Madness, Two Tone and other Doc-saturated subcultures as young kids; now that they were in bands themselves, they

↓

Right: Blur, one of the pivotal Britpop bands of the '90s. Their Anglo-centric stance necessarily adopted the 1460.

No Doubt

Perhaps the most high profile of all the stars to have emerged from the so-called third wave of ska in America is No Doubt's lead vocalist, Gwen Stefani.

Revered – and occasionally reviled – for her unique combination of street style and haute couture, Stefani's sartorial chic is all her own. From over-sized personalized jewellery and two-tone dog-tooth suits – best seen on No Doubt's 'Hey Baby' and Stefani's collaboration with Eve, entitled 'Let Me Blow Ya Mind' – to the more punk-influenced bondage trousers of the 1997 breakthrough single, 'Don't Speak', her look is nothing if not unique. Part of that look has consistently been a pair of Dr. Martens – a legacy of Stefani's formative influences, which are deeply rooted in the British Two-Tone scene of the late '80s.

Born in 1969 (thus at the tail end of that decade of 'Love and Peace', of the Fab Four and of man on the moon), Stefani was brought up a Catholic in Orange County, southern California, with her brothers Eric and Todd and her sister Jill. Playing the piccolo in her school band and performing water ballet were just two of her earliest musical experiences. In contrast to her famously lithe physique in No Doubt, Gwen insists that as a young girl she was 'fat all over'.

A pre-pubescent fascination with movie soundtracks such as *The Sound of Music*, *Muppet Movie* and *Annie* was quickly superseded by a growing interest in the ska records being played by her brother Eric. Top of the play list were The Specials, Selecter and Madness; all bands born out of grim, English inner-city decay and boasting a musical and stylistic potency that struck a chord with the young Stefani. In actual fact, the second wave of British ska in the late '70s enjoyed only limited commercial success in America, although bands like Her Majesties Secret Service did bring the Two-Tone sound to the US in the early '80s. This Anglo-centric focus was readily complemented by vinyl from more colloquial acts such as LA's The Untouchables and Fishbone.

It was Madness who made the biggest impact on Stefani, who started dressing as a ska girl at Loara High School. Despite this, when she first sang publicly (dressed as Julie Andrews at a talent show with Eric) she sang The Selecter's 'On My Radio'. Stefani was only seventeen when she formed No Doubt with her keyboard-playing brother Eric and his friend John Spence, a black ska punk, the latter holding joint vocals with her. This wasn't the first time she and Eric had shown artistic aspirations; their joint performing career dated back to when brother and sister would put on puppet shows for their neighbours.

Stefani's solo singing role came about only after John Spence committed suicide in December 1987. With the subsequent recruitment of Indian-born Tony Kanal (with whom Stefani had a seven-year

romance, chronicled in the smash single 'Don't Speak'), guitarist Tom Dumont and drummer Adrian Young, the line-up was complete. For a considerable length of time, the story of No Doubt was one of toil and under-achievement. For eight years the band struggled to establish its own identity and sound around the countless small clubs in and around Anaheim, California. The vogue for angst-filled rock and cod-punk made this task even more problematic. A debut album (entitled *No Doubt*) filled with ska-pop fusion sank almost without trace amid the global fascination with grunge and 'loser' culture. The band's own disillusionment was matched by a sceptical record company, making the future of No Doubt look bleak.

Stiffening their resolve, the band self-funded the recording and release of a new record, *Beacon Street Collection*, the project that saw them turn the corner. Steady progress was made until the release of their third long-player – 1995's Grammy-nominated *Tragic Kingdom* – at which point No Doubt turned into one of the biggest acts on the planet. By this stage, Stefani's brother, Eric, had left the band to work

as an animator on *The Simpsons* (No Doubt's early logos and artwork were his creations).

The success of that record plus the 'comeback' album, *The Return of Saturn*, in 2000 has kept the highly photogenic and media-friendly Stefani firmly in the spotlight for years. Her ongoing relationship with Bush's Gavin Rossdale has made the pair one of music's most photographed couples. The 'G' necklace that Stefani famously wears is actually a tribute to her boyfriend/fiancé Gavin rather than – as is often mistakenly assumed – for herself.

A self-proclaimed 'thrift-store junkie', Stefani's interest in clothes and fashion has extended to her own line of clothes, to be launched in 2004 under the label L.A.M.B. She has been designing her own stage clothes since the start of the band's career, aided in this by her major in art from Cal State Fullerton College, which she attended after she graduated from high school. She is famous for making her own outfits and traces this back to when her own mother made her a replica of the dress worn by Maria in *The Sound of Music* for a high-school talent show. In the past, Stefani has used the services of designer Debra Viereck.

Such individuality has made Stefani something of an iconic fashion peculiarity, particularly in a world where, increasingly, the homogenous and bland are prevalent. She seems able to morph seamlessly from Marilyn Monroe pastiches to punk die-hard, from '40s silver-screen starlet to ska purist, to high-fashion guru. Likewise, her hairstyles have mutated from the original platinum-blonde ponytail to outrageous red-and-blonde plaits and even a partially dreadlocked nest.

Vampish, bee-stung red lipstick, bindis on her forehead, crop tops, quirky hats and chunky shoes complete the look. She somehow blends Doris Day, Shirley Temple, Madonna, Catwoman and Siouxsie Sioux all into one – yet all with lashings of Stefani flavour. This in turn has inspired thousands of fans to dress as so-called 'Gwennabes'.

The media have focussed on this image to such an extent that, at one point, the band ended up refusing to do cover shoots unless all four members were included. Described by some as a perfect blend of little-girl-lost innocence and riot-girl feminism, Stefani wore a pair of red DM's on the cover of *Tragic Kingdom*; her collection of Docs contains many customized pairs.

> "In our minds we were making reasonably left-field, arty pop music. And yet we were getting screamed at as if we were a bunch of tough guys singing ballads with a dance routine."

Dave Rowntree of Blur, on the *Parklife* hysteria

emulated their heroes, and were in turn aped by their own generation of followers. This is a classic example of the self-perpetuating cycle of influence that has effectively kept Doc Martens at the heart of every subculture, virtually since the boot's inception.

Over the next splendid eighteen months, Pulp finally broke their fourteen-year duck and produced a sexually subversive, comically seedy masterpiece; this was their first major label album, *His 'n' Hers*. Elastica, the Auteurs and the soon-to-be global Radiohead all also made an impact. Supergrass' debut album, *I Should Coco*, hit No. 1 and a litany of other bands enjoyed

Left: Oasis, 'best band in the world', according to Noel Gallagher.

purple patches as well, including Shed Seven, Portishead, The Bluetones, Marion and Dodgy.

The mod movement enjoyed an indirect boost and mini-revival as well, with the so-called 'Modfather', Paul Weller, enjoying some of his biggest successes to date. Elsewhere, live music experienced a resurgence, band-merchandise sales rocketed, festivals were repeatedly sold out and record shops couldn't stock enough of Britpop acts.

Unfortunately, the international appeal of these bands was limited. It goes without saying that Oasis, the latecomers who took all the honors, enjoyed huge success worldwide. (The Gallagher boys were rarely seen in Docs, tending to wear the desert boot.) This was also the case for one of

their support bands who came good, The Verve. Generally, however, America found the ironic and quirky Britpop scene rather unappealing.

Back in Britain, Britpop couldn't last, of course. By the time Blur and Oasis were engaging in their fêted battle for the No. 1 slot in August 1995, there were already dissenters who bemoaned the mainstream prostitution of the scene, just like glam, punk, grunge and many others before it. By mid '96, with most of the big Britpop players recording new material or on sabbaticals, the movement was effectively dead.

As with many musical movements, the most accomplished, original and innovative players had the ability to transcend the genre with which they were – often reluctantly – associated. This was clearly the case with Blur, Suede and the Manic Street Preachers. While they were quickly tagged at the time by a Britpop-hungry media, their music since the mid '90s has shown that they are creatively complex and artistically progressive.

Blur's eponymous fifth album was a dramatic shift in direction, with its hardcore-influenced abrasive guitars and thunderous rhythm section (best shown in the classic 'Song 2') winning major acclaim. Suede overcame the loss of their guitarist and returned with the quite brilliant, chart-topping long player Coming Up, which was crammed with both classic singles and deeper, more pensive album tracks. The Manic Street Preachers similarly suffered the loss of a member (the tragic disappearance of Richey Edwards) but have since released some superb albums – most poignantly, perhaps, with their universally revered This Is My Truth Tell Me Yours.

Ska revival

One American phenomenon of the late '90s that can be traced directly back to precisely the kind of British heritage in which Docs have been so heavily immersed is the ska revival, led by bands such as No Doubt.

   This scene was itself preceded by a more underground wave of bands, including Weaker Youth Ensemble, the Allstonians, Bim Skala Bim, the Voodoo Glow Skulls and The Toasters. This last band once called itself Not Bob Marley, and its members have been instrumental in boosting the popularity of ska music in the US. Referred to by observers as 'the third wave of

ska', this movement started evolving into a commercial behemoth in 1996 when, alongside No Doubt, came bands like Smash Mouth, Goldfinger and Reel Big Fish. These bands' multiplatinum success took ska-influenced music to commercially enormous heights.

   Purists aired their grievances as to the viability of some of these bands' variants on the originals, apparently ignoring the fact that the very essence of the musical underground is that each new generation takes from its own environment and makes of it something new and uniquely its own.

   The huge success of bands such as these provided a genuine alternative to the post-grunge rock bands that were filling MTV's schedules. Most interesting of all was their eclectic mix of influences – not just ska, but also metal, hardcore, hip-hop and even classical music have been used to great effect by this new wave of musicians. Just as the Two-Tone phenomenon had provided a glimpse of British youth at the turn of the '80s, so this third wave showed just how multicultural and varied the American youth of the '90s had become. Not surprisingly, with bands drawing on such disparate

ideas, styles and music, Docs were bound to crop up. The influence of Madness, Bad Manners, British punk bands, mods and even skinhead music was prevalent and rapidly assimilated by this new wave of culture-hungry kids. Hence, two or even three decades after the original British cults found Docs on their feet, the boots and shoes were being pulled on by Americans of a younger generation.

   Bands such as No Doubt frequently showcased themselves on the flourishing festival circuit that reached its zenith in the '90s. The modern festival, with its corporate sponsorship, webcasts and heavily merchandised product, is a highly polished version (apart from the lavatories!) of a basic concept that had started life decades previously.

   Cultural historians argue over the exact birth of the festival phenomenon. Suffice to say that most agree that the Monterey Pop Festival in 1967 can claim to be one of the earliest, if not the first, such event. With The Who and a guitar-burning Jimi Hendrix on top form, it was little wonder that in the aftermath of this seminal concert other

Right: US ska champs Smashmouth.

"I regarded the whole thing as a cross between a harvest festival and a pop festival."

Michael Eavis, founder of Glastonbury Festival

promoters, and also fans, looked for more of the same.

The '90s in Britain, mainland Europe and America witnessed a glut of festivals, all of which seemed to be capable of enticing hundreds of thousands of music-lovers to increasingly cramped and muddy fields. There, to stand shoulder to shoulder with thousands of others for a weekend, to sleep (badly) in a tent, urinate in conditions to which the grazing cows would object and pay extortionate prices for a plate of cold chips.

Hence the remarkable success of Glastonbury, Reading and Leeds, the 'V' festivals and America's Lollapalooza, the Tibetan Freedom shows and the Warped tour, all of which – for a good run of time – sold out year after year. Further afield, shows such as Australia's Big Day Out mirrored the global popularity of the festival phenomenon.

Left: Sleeping arrangements at the Glastonbury Festival.

The enigmatic organizer of Glastonbury, farmer Michael Eavis (himself a loyal DM's wearer), booked the very first festival at this West Country location in the autumn of 1970; he did so entirely on his own and with no prior knowledge of the music business. The Kinks headlined and were paid £500. In more recent times, the same headline slot could comfortably generate £500,000.

At that first Glastonbury festival back in September 1970, Eavis handed out free milk and provided a large ox roast (which was hijacked by hungry Hells Angels). He still lost £1,500. However, even this festival – the granddaddy of British festivals – became plagued in the late '90s and early '00s with problems over licenses, due to over-crowding and safety issues.

Alongside annual events like Glastonbury are 'one-off' festivals such as Woodstock and Live Aid. Famously, Woodstock organizers and police underestimated attendance at the 'free' show in Bethel, upstate New York, by about 800,000; notably, these 'Three Days of Peace And Music' witnessed three deaths, two births and four miscarriages.

Festivals are no longer just hours and hours of music you can't hear properly. The original simplistic format has evolved into a showcase for countless 'worthy' causes such as anti-racism, gay liberation, animal rights, the homeless and scores of charitable and other issues. Stalls at respective sites might include major and minor protest groups, such as Greenpeace, gun-control lobbyists and civil liberties groups.

Due to the frequent mud baths that festivals invariably create, Docs have become a staple item in any festival-goer's bag for the weekend. In the late '80s in the UK, when the so-called grebo scene was dominating the alternative landscape, Reading was awash with both mud and 1460s. Similarly, in 1992, when Nirvana played at the same festival amid backstage rumors that Kurt Cobain was using heroin again, a generation of grunge kids paraded their eight-holers in similar quantities. As the thousands of kids trudged home, with their boots ↓

Travellers

The British traveller is generally regarded to have begun life around the time of the 1974 Stonehenge People's Free Festival, which itself was a descendant of the Isle of Wight festivals of the previous decade.

In 1970, the Windsor Free Festival was covered in the squatters' slogan 'Pay No Rent', while other events around this time saw similar daubs applied by like-minded individuals.

Key figures such as Sid Rawles, Bill Ubique Dwyer, Dr John and Wally Hope were instrumental in creating the free festival movement, often inspired by slogans imported from America's West Coast, themselves a legacy of the Haight-Ashbury days of San Francisco in the late '60s. This loved-up vibe evolved in the '70s into a more proactive political slant. British travellers often looked much farther back in history, to English activists of the 1600s and to writers such as Gerrard Winstanley of the Diggers, who tried to reclaim common land for the oppressed.

Many travelling festival-goers soon made the natural progression to an entire lifestyle on the road, creating mobile mini-societies as they roamed the countryside. Inevitably, this led to clashes with society and the establishment. One such perennial flashpoint was Stonehenge, the prehistoric monument that saw its first Summer Solstice festival in 1974, instigated by Wally Hope. His group squatted at the site for most of that year. Now Stonehenge is run by English Heritage, and visitors have to buy a ticket in order to access the stone circle; a decision that has evoked many angry protests and clashes with police.

Many travelling communities have been the targets of both hysterical media coverage and oppressive government legislation in recent times (in particular, via the Criminal Justice Bill of 1994, which attempted to restrict gatherings

in public). This is in spite of the fact that most travellers are entirely pacific and self-sufficient, with education, work, recreation and social facilities of their own. Nevertheless, newspapers such as the *Daily Telegraph* still deemed it necessary to call them 'a swarming tribe of human locusts'. This media and establishment hysteria is nothing new – at the 1975 Windsor Free festival, seven picnickers, five onlookers, nine journalists and four welfare organizations were watched over by 350 riot police.

"Doc Martens boots have become phenomenally popular throughout the teenage population [reflecting] the basic traveller's wardrobe."

Extract from *A Time To Travel* by Fiona Earle et al.

> "Willis Elf is wearing a pair of Doc Martens which have been painted and decorated with a constellation of silver stars. These stars are already disappearing behind a nebula of mud. Such is the detrimental effect of being in this place that I am now capable of holding a conversation with a man who calls himself Willis Elf and paints stars on his boots, and not minding too much. A very poor state for me to be in."

Martin Millar, from his novel *Love and Peace with Melody Paradise*

spattered in mud and their hands full of flyers, they did not know that this was the last time that Kurt Cobain and Nirvana would ever perform in England.

Unfortunately, by the end of the decade, the mud-loving festival-goer had reached saturation point, resulting in several high-profile cancellations of entire festivals. When the Queen held her own Jubilee festival at Buckingham Palace in 2002, with Brian May performing a surreal guitar solo on top of the palace and thousands of fans – of all musical persuasions – swarming all over Her Majesty's flowerbeds, it seemed perhaps that the alternative ethos and appeal of the festival had gone forever. Yet somehow the best festivals remain a compelling spectacle – and perhaps they always will.

The 'weekend traveller' seen at festivals, who might return to his suit and tie on the Monday morning, was a far cry from the legion of people who lived this lifestyle every waking minute of their lives. A mainly – and peculiarly – British conceit, the traveller came to the attention of the media in the '90s.

Public prominence was achieved via a combination of high-profile protests at green-belt road developments and a popularization of traveller-fashion and ideals (intentionally or otherwise) through such bands as The Levellers (a band regularly associated with travellers) and Back to the Planet. These bands were reluctantly tarred with the unsavoury tag of 'crusties'.

The Levellers' members were frequently seen wearing DM's. Formed in the south of England in the coastal town of Brighton, Sussex, their mix of folk instrumentation and rock and punk ethics proved a popular melting pot of ideas. 'We draw on some Celtic influences because it's a powerful source, but we're a very English band.' Their *Levelling The Land* album in 1991 was a huge commercial success in the UK, backed by an

Right: The mud bath, a festival staple.

enigmatic live following that was famed for its unswerving loyalty. The band's name and ideology was inspired by a group of political activists called the Levellers, who had set about challenging the status quo at the time of the English Civil War in the mid 1600s.

The last few years of the '90s saw the emergence of yet another dominant US music genre – so-called nu-metal (initially called rapcore, this latter term was quickly dropped in favour of nu-metal). Spearheaded by Limp Bizkit, whose frontman Fred Durst became one of the most powerful men in the music industry, this scene was a massive commercial hit in 1998 and 1999.

Nu-metal could trace its most recent roots back to the Deftones and most obviously Korn, both of whose debut albums set a precedent for latter-day nu-metal. Scouring music's history books suggests that this was an inevitable fusion of rap and metal, taking the vocal delivery of the former with the headlong, over-driven guitar surges of the latter.

Even bands such as Led Zeppelin and Black Sabbath

Left: The Levellers.

could rightly lay claim to having sown some of the seeds of success that nu-metal was reaping – others might suggest that the inception of nu-metal began when Aerosmith and Run DMC cooperated on their aforementioned 1986 classic, 'Walk This Way'. Almost any track by Rage Against The Machine might also offer hints of nu-metal's evolution. Whatever the exact genealogical origins, this predominantly white and American music (with a few exceptions, such as the British West Country's A) proved to be hugely commercial.

Limp Bizkit were initially the biggest act from the scene, selling over over ten million copies of their excellent *Chocolate Starfish and the Hot Dog Flavoured Water* album. Latterly, the somewhat more contrived Linkin Park released what was the biggest-selling album of 2001 with *Hybrid Theory*. Their detractors claimed that, for all of their posturing, they were little more than a manufactured act and no better than a boy band, but such criticisms were harsh and seemed of little consequence. After all, with chart hip-hop delving into misogyny and cliché, and the onslaught of manufactured pop just around

the corner, for many nu-metal was the only viable alternative.

Nu-metal fans and bands wore their baseball caps back to front (Durst's famous red cap was the most obvious example), with goatee beards, their pants extra baggy and hooded tops over a T-shirt, itself worn over a long-sleeved top. DM's did find some popularity, although not as much as the sneaker did. The fringes of the scene attracted some former metal heads, and here the 1460 was commonplace.

Into a new era

As the world hurtled toward the turn of a new century, the Millennium Bug struck fear deep into the heart of society. This fact of a simple date on a computer chip resulted in much trepidation. While computer wizards all over the globe charged themselves out at emergency 'overnight millionaire' rates, all the world could do was sit and wait for the clock to tick over . . . and nothing at all to happen.

The end of the '90s saw Dr. Martens approaching its 40th anniversary established as one of the most iconic items in fashion history. Oddly enough, despite the mass of corporate branding, advertising, products on offer and a generally buoyant

> "When we examined the boot closely we found a tiny cut in the leather and two lumps in my foot . . . two bits of metal pierced the leather at such speed that the leather had actually closed back over the entrance points. There is still a bit of bullet in my foot. I bought those boots some time ago when I was sent to cover the Gulf War."

News reporter Kate Adie in Bosnia

consumer economy, the fashions of the late '90s were becoming increasingly homogenous. Your favourite pop star might easily be seen on the front cover of a glossy magazine wearing the same jacket as your father's favourite rocker. The era of 'wild haircuts' seemed to have faded as the high street became a blur of the bland.

Similarly, although with more positive effects, musical genres had become so intertwined and self-referential that few new bands could genuinely create a fashion craze. Acts such as Slipknot inspired their fans to wear boiler suits and boots (often DM's), but this was very much a small clique of hardcore followers and certainly not a national fad.

Some people argued that the Internet had made socializing the domain of the anonymous – providing a place where individuals from across the planet could share common interests without ever meeting one another in person. This inevitably diluted the impact of a certain look or style, and rendered the act of frequenting a particular club – as so many subcultures had done in the past – less significant. A bedroom geek could sit in isolation and be a goth, a punk, a psychobilly. . . or anything at all.

Added to this was an old fashion obsession taken to fresh extremes. It seemed that celebrities were now the ultimate oracles of influence. The late Princess Diana had inspired a million haircuts and imitation designer gowns; soon Jennifer Aniston replaced her as the most-requested coiffure, with English soccer captain David Beckham doing the same for the male population.

Celebrity magazines such as *Heat* and *OK!* enjoyed record sales as the cult of the television and movie celebrity shifted the focus of a generation away from the gig circuit. Reinforcing this evolution was the still novel phenomenon of 'reality TV' – with pop stars chosen by the public, created for TV and inseparable from the cult of celebrity. The challenge facing Dr. Martens – and all fashion and shoe brands – in the new millennium was that of how to assert identity in an increasingly monochrome and saccharine media culture.

Right: Slipknot.

It started with an anti-climax, as the old millennium disappeared and the new one was ushered in minus the global meltdown of the much-hyped 'millennium bug'. The new era saw the self-perpetuating cycle of fashion and musical reinvention throw up an entirely fresh generation of icons. In the thick of the melting pot once more was Dr. Martens, now forty years young.

2000
onward

A participant in the Burning Man Festival, Nevada

2000 onward

The avoidance of an Armageddon-style global meltdown courtesy of the Millennium Bug meant that the second millennium passed into the third with a relieved slither rather than a catastrophic bang.

With the 9/11 horror of the Twin Towers of New York being razed to the ground by hijacked airliners crammed with hundreds of passengers and tonnes of aviation fuel, the fight against terrorism took on an altogether new meaning. While America assisted in the downfall of the Taliban in Afghanistan, Osama Bin Laden was nowhere to be found. Meanwhile, politicians debated the measures that might be taken in the event of whole cities being wiped out by weapons of mass destruction. It all amounted to a terrifying start to a new era.

In America, the public was divided between those who backed the 'Texan cowboy', George W. Bush, and those who shied away from conflict. In the UK, New Labour's honeymoon period was most definitely over, with Tony Blair failing to maintain anywhere near the record popularity he once held, caught in a mire of asylum hysteria, transport chaos and backbench rebellion by Labour MPs. Despite the British economy remaining proudly buoyant in the face of growing global uncertainty, the British public seemed already to be losing patience with the Blairite vision of the UK.

By the year 2000, the Internet was a fact of life for most in the Western world. Indeed, while the 'dotcom' bubble had burst and sent tech shares and Web listings such as Nasdaq plummeting, there were still certain areas of the Web that appeared to make financial sense. After an initial period deep in the red, Amazon established itself as arguably the most successful Internet brand, a title that the hugely successful auction site e-bay would surely challenge.

One other site, however, attracted even more attention – Napster. Started as a site for sharing digital music files, Napster was rapidly seen as a grave threat to the future existence of the music industry. Why spend millions of dollars developing and releasing new music when Net friends would swap the product free of charge months in advance of its street release? Eventually, the normally isolationist record company major labels joined forces and Napster was curtailed. Nonetheless, this was the perfect example of the changing face of post-2000 business and culture.

By the turn of the new millennium, subcultures as we

**Right: (clockwise from top left)
Bush declares 'War on Terror'; dotcom
shares crash; the Internet, now a way of
life; the devastating after-effects of 9/11.**

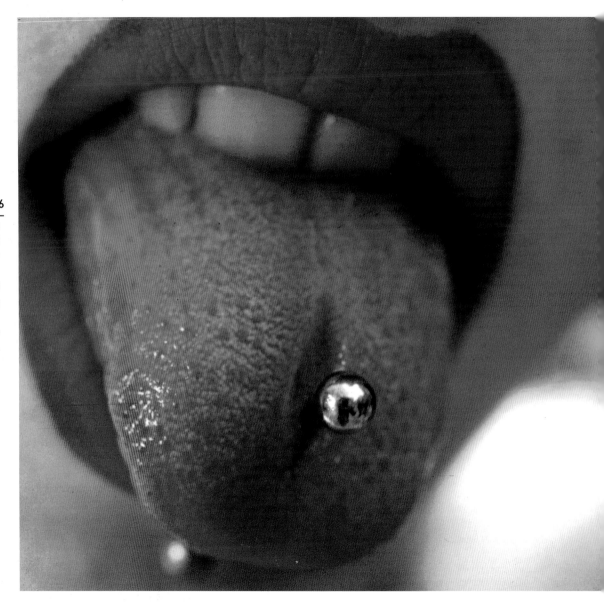

"Technology is like a fish. The longer it stays on the shelf, the less desirable it becomes."

IBM exec. bemoaning the slow progress of computer technology

had known them in previous decades had altered beyond recognition. Some sceptics even suggested they no longer existed. The blurring of styles and dress codes across an increasingly broad range of age groups, economic strata and musical tastes did, at times, give the impression that bland was the new black. Not so. You only had to scratch beneath the surface to see that the tribal mentality still existed – and exists today.

The skinhead is a good example of a youth culture that has evolved exponentially since its early '60s inception. Back then, clippers were set to grade four; by the late '70s this was usually grade two or one; by 2000, the dark shadow was popular again. The original monkey and cheap working-man's boots were, as previously highlighted, replaced by eight-eyelet Dr. Martens, mostly in

Left: Piercing is more popular in what have been dubbed the 'Noughties'.

oxblood; the '80s saw the ten-holer take over and later the fourteen-holer also became very popular.

Trousers have evolved from bleached red-tag Levi's to combats in grey or green camouflage. Levi's worn by post-2000 skins are rarely bleached. Smart skin wear is still the tonik suit, usually worn with loafers or brogues. Braces started off with a width of two inches yet most recently worn are those with a five-inch width. Skins in the '60s did not tend to have ear pierces; '70s skins sported a single pierce, often a stud; '80s skins quite often preferred one pierce in each ear. Notably, skins from Sunderland were seen wearing nose rings as early the start of the '70s – years before punks adopted the look. For most skins, the Dr. Martens boot still reigns supreme.

Of course, the original skinheads were defiantly working class. So it is perhaps an anomaly that such credence should be given to wearing

Also in 2000

- 8.2 billion e-mails are sent worldwide.

- *Gladiator*, starring Russell Crowe, woos critics at the Oscars.

- The most performed song of the twentieth century is declared to be 'Happy Birthday'.

- Wary technology investors cause stocks to plunge, signalling the beginning of the end of the Internet stock boom.

- The mass murder (or suicide?) of hundreds associated with the Doomsday Cult is uncovered in a village in Uganda, western Africa.

- A Concorde crash kills 113 at Charles de Gaulle airport, just outside Paris.

Also in 2001

- The first episode in the long-awaited cinematic epic, *Lord of the Rings – The Fellowship of the Ring*, premiers.

- Britain is gripped by a livestock endemic of foot and mouth disease, crippling the farming community.

- The September 11 attacks leave the world reeling; shortly after, President Bush declares the 'War on Terror'.

> "Our Age of Anxiety is, in great part, the result of trying to do today's jobs with yesterday's tools."

Marshall McLuhan

exactly the right labels, which can often be expensive. Cultural commentator Dassos Stassoulli has written regarding this: 'The greatest thing about the skinhead look is that it was more about attitude than clothes. Having its roots in poor working-class [culture] meant that instead of fancy labels and a fixed style, one wore what was affordable in a certain manner.'

Despite such reservations, all of the above sartorial developments are a perfect example of how subcultures never stand still. Yet the skin culture has undergone an even more drastic mutation in the closing years of the twentieth century – into gay culture. While the straight '90s skinhead frequently veered off into wearing Adidas trainers with other labels, such as Kappa and Umbro tracksuits, the emergence of the skin look in gay culture harked back to the epitome of the skinhead image.

Combat fatigues (green or grey) were extremely popular, while the hair was kept very short, either a grade one or a dark shadow. The flying jacket was the preferred coat of choice, while Dr. Martens were almost universal. Sometimes, a small mohican-style ridge was left to grow on the middle of the head, aping the punk look of two decades previously. This tuft of hair was similarly often dyed in a variety of colours. This diversion from the '60s skins was encouraged by the adoption of the cropped haircut by many high-profile celebrities, with David Beckham and Ewan McGregor – both of whom have large gay followings – championing the look. It seemed that a look that was formerly a fashion pariah was now a mainstream essential.

Some gay circles took the style one step further, adopting a de facto dress code. Some of the more sartorially strict gay skin clubs would even turn away customers who were not dressed correctly. Either way, the look became immensely popular within the gay underground. Indeed, it has even evolved into a genuine fetish scene, with emphasis placed on such elements as the size of the actual boots – with the bigger the Dr. Martens, the bigger the attraction.

Inevitably, the adoption of the look within gay culture upset some skinheads. Obviously, whether a skin was gay or straight, black or white actually had no relevance to the original ethics of the multiracial liberality of the movement's origins. Some sections of the skin community took exception, however, and began dressing in a different fashion so as to be discernible from the gay skin. Such individuals deplored the fact that many gay skins had no concept of the original music and lifestyle patterns of the movement, and were using the look purely as a superficial fashion statement.

The derogatory term 'fashion skin' was thus coined to designate those with cropped haircuts that formed part of this latest evolution. Interestingly, many gay skins reacted by tucking the AirWair heel tag out of sight inside the boot, and also

Right: Heavy boots have become part of the gay 'uniform'.

289

2000 onward

making their laces similarly inconspicuous, thereby asserting their own identity as being at the opposite extreme to that of straight, traditional skins. Such opposing tendencies make it all the more remarkable that the Dr. Martens boot enjoys almost universal appeal, and is still favoured by most strands within the skinhead culture as a whole.

Notably, this mentality of 'exclusivity' was not confined to those who were outside the gay skin culture, looking in. Within the community itself, there were splinter groups, often demarcated by sexual preference. Hence there are 'S&M Skins', 'Water sports Skins', 'Army Skins' and so on. The colour code of laces is also used on occasion, with red denoting S&M and yellow suggesting a preference for 'watersports'.

Whatever the rival factions within the skinhead movement, their existence alone is ample evidence of the ongoing vitality and complexity of tribal subculture. In some ways, this internal conflict within an underground movement reflects, in a microcosm, the rivalry between so many other tribes –

Left: Coloured laces can indicate a preference for S&M or 'watersports'.

for example, between revivalist mods and scooter boys in the early '80s and between mods and rockers in the '60s. In short, between just about every youth subculture and its inevitable polar opposite. Such antithetical styles and ethics are the very fuel that burns at the heart of each tribe.

Skaters

One tribe that Dr. Martens has traditionally struggled to infiltrate is the skater culture. Originating back in the '70s, urban myth suggests that the first skateboard was a '50s surfboard melded onto roller skates by a frustrated surfer. By contrast, the craze of the late '70s was utterly mainstream, possessing few of the traits of a subculture. However, when the authorities began banning skaters from public places and areas where skate skills could be shown off became few and far between, the fad turned in on itself and headed underground.

At this early stage, skaters resembled surfers with baggy trousers (themselves a reaction to the skin-tight leggings of rollerbladers) and colourful T-shirts. For this activity, the footwear of choice was never Dr. Martens. Other brands such as Vans were commonplace. ↓

Also in 2002

- DVD technology becomes commonplace within the home.

- The US search for Osama Bin Laden is paralleled by a growing intolerance of Iraqi leader Saddam Hussein's regime. UN weapons inspectors are allowed back into the country, with the purpose of hunting out Iraq's alleged 'Weapons of Mass Destruction'.

- The UK housing market is booming, seeing the value of some homes increase by as much as 50 per cent in a year, prompting fears of a potential crash similar to that which occurred during the '80s.

- Plasma TV screens emerge. Although extortionately priced, they sell heavily.

- *Star Wars: Attack Of the Clones* is the first big budget film to be shot with digital cameras.

- MTV reportedly now reaches 250 million homes worldwide.

- DVD burners are now widely used for downloading movies.

Betty Jackson

"I wanted to highlight the juxtaposition between hard and soft by adding transparent rouched chiffon and ribbon."

> ## "Let him who would enjoy a good future waste none of his present."

Roger Babson

Partly because they held more kudos in skate circles, but principally because DM's were simply too heavy, rigid and incapable of gripping the board. In skate magazines such as *Thrasher*, the DM's boot was nowhere to be seen.

When punk came onto the scene, its urban nihilism appealed more to skaters than it did to the 'back-to-nature' surfers, and so skater punk was born. Although some aspects of punk fashion appealed, the styles were either diluted or dumped. Once again, individual and 'thrift-store chic' were the flavour of the day. Some writers have even suggested that skater-punk style actually laid the foundations for the birth of the grunge look.

Elements of over-sized hip-hop styling leaked into skate wear; more recently, the latter look, together with its associated extreme music, have also veered off into the similar – albeit snow-covered – terrain of

Left: DM's have struggled to capture support from within skater culture.

snowboarding. How the Dr. Martens boot came to enjoy a small but significant slice of this complex and only loosely grouped genre was through the ceaseless intermingling of seemingly opposite factions within youth culture. As the punk and grunge music enjoyed by these different sections became increasingly similar, so some of their stylistic interests also began to merge.

By the late '90s, a plethora of US bands was touring the globe that drew in elements of punk, skater style and ska influences. By now, many of these bands could in no way be seen as skater punk; instead, they were an idiosyncratic blend of a multitude of influences. The West Coast band Reel Big Fish is the most obvious example. More accurately, RBF were actually ska-punk and, along with similar bands such as Goldfinger and the record label Mojo, this scene enjoyed substantial popularity.

At the heart of Reel Big Fish's amalgamated look were DM's, and these were frequently

cherry-red. Having said that, though, the Doc will never be the mainstay of skate punk, although the splinter groups and individualism exhibited by such tribes can often find a place for the plain 1460.

40th anniversary

The 40th anniversary of the inception of the 1460 Dr. Martens boot fell, of course, on 1 April 2000. To celebrate the milestone – something which few brands thus deeply embedded within youth culture can boast – DM's held a number of celebrations, including an exhibition at the famous Design Museum in Shad Thames, next to the Tower Bridge in London. The aforementioned secret gig by Madness was itself complemented by a 40-track CD compilation with Virgin Records, which typified the breadth of influence the brand has had during these 40 years.

The ongoing presence of Dr. Martens in the very fabric of youth culture is guaranteed by the continuing cyclical nature of new music. The biggest new band of the twenty-first century – The Strokes – are a fine example of how music and youth culture are constantly reinventing the past for a new generation. Themselves a

> "The fear of becoming a 'has-been' keeps some people from becoming anything."

Eric Hoffer, *The Passionate State of the Mind*, 1954

walking homage to the Velvet Underground, The Strokes became an instant hit with the fashionista and style press from the moment they appeared on the scene in 2001. Admired in equal measures for their dishevelled look and their straight-down-the-line punk pop, The Strokes were seen in some magazine photo shoots wearing DM's, which some observers felt were the perfect anchor for their ultra-cool look.

The parallels with the Velvets are obvious and numerous – from the shades and the leather jackets to the all-black clothes and the scruffy hair. Clearly, Lou Reed's outfit didn't wear DM's during their zenith in the late '60s, but the shoes nonetheless fit seamlessly into the referential look so stylishly adopted by The Strokes. Other New York bands lumped in by the media with The Strokes in 2001 included such outfits as The White Stripes, The Vines, The Hives, The Coral, The Libertines and The Black Rebel Motorcycle Club. Many of these acts also wore DM's.

The continued championing of the classic boot by new bands and their fans is proof positive of the continual reinvention of Dr. Martens. Thus an unlikely fashion icon can begin to enjoy a new generation of fans. Dr. Martens have, inadvertently, attained a status and cultural significance that could never have been foreseen on their launch in April 1960.

Almost from the outset, DM's have won a diverse allegiance from an incredible array of subcultures. With each shift in youth fashion and thought, new generations have moulded the shoe and recycled it for their own ends, each time injecting it with a new 'underground' potency which, in turn, has been mimicked by the next generation – heaping yet more heritage on its unassuming shape. Even in this new millennium, where the media blurs the boundaries between subcultures so that they succeed one another with frightening speed, Doc Martens still appear to hold their own.

The original 1460 is clearly a modern design classic. Internationally, there is only a handful of designs that can boast similar status: Ray Bans, Levi's, the VW Beetle, Zippo Lighters, Marlboro cigarettes, and the black leather jacket. In Britain, the list is far smaller: the Mini motorcar, Fred Perrys. What was once a plain workwear boot is now a good-looking subcultural essential. It has become the perfect marriage of form and fashion. With bands such as The Strokes donning the black 1460 with enthusiasm, this unlikely fashion icon has a new generation of fans.

Dr. Martens are one of the oddest fashion trends of all time. They go with boiler suits, combats, pinstripes, bondage trousers or flowery dresses. They will probably be around as long as people have feet. They have always annoyed your parents. They remain the first and only boot of their kind on the market. Like the subcultures that created them, they are scruffy, smart, sexy, macho, fashionable, fashionless, classy, classless, uniform, unique. They are, quite simply, Dr. Martens.

Right: The Strokes.

I Pay Homage to...
Doc Martens

Being a closet goth, I have an insatiable appetite for gawd-awful ugly shoes. I lust after Doc Martens. When it comes to clothing products I have incredible brand loyalty, to which my Doc collection serves as a proud testament. My Doc-wearing history started in 1992 with the acquisition of two classic pairs of Docs, one pair of shoes, and one pair of boots. They were kindly shipped over from Swansea, Wales, by Catte. The shoes came from an Army surplus store in Swansea, and the boots were kindly broken in by Mike, a semi-anonymous Swansea Doc stomper. Anyone who has broken in Docs can appreciate the significance of receiving pre-broken-in boots. These two pairs have served me faithfully, but in 1997 I had the kind fortune, and cash, to complement my collection with several new pairs.

I bought my third and fourth pair of Docs in Camden Town, London, in January and July 1997. The third pair are T-strap Mary-Janes in black (of course).

The fourth pair are classic steel-toed shoes.

Having gigantic flipper feet, being nearly six feet tall, and laboring through average sizeness means I'm generally tough on my shoes. They must be comfortable, they must be durable, and they must be practical. Docs are all of those and more. From the famous bouncing soles to the durable welted uppers, Docs have successfully stomped me through numerous raves and clubs, frozen Ottawa streets, fashionable London alleys, and the backwaters of muddy Mississippi, with nary a scratch. Okay, so the right sole on my '92 classic shoes is splitting, if you were a five-year-old pair of abused Docs you would split too! I love my Docs!

by Kirstin A. Hargie, 1998

Hi. I'd just like to say that, umm, I adore my Docs... all the pairs I have. My first pair – black 8 ups – I got over, umm, five years ago... and my proudest achievement is wearing them for 14 days straight (this includes sleeping in them and also walking a lot). Which I still have and wear to this very day. I also have a pair of blue 8 ups, which I wear not as frequently but just when I want to be different. I have worn Docs my whole life as does my Dad and everyone in my family. My dogs would wear them too if they could...

Web posting sourced by the author, 1998

Dr. Martens – The Story of an Icon

My Dr. Martens

I own a pair of boots, a pair of Dr. Martens yeah I do,

And every time I wear them I feel so brand new,

Elated by and hooked on their ability to make me look better than you,

Yes ego gets a real boost but not just any old pair of shoes mind you,

Been around since 1960 and they still shine too,

Still top of the line too,

When I'm in my DM's I'm pleased,

These are the D's in it's been a DM good day,

The M's in much more manageable than blue suede,

My top of the range Goodyear Welted construction and heat-sealed soles,

Are designed so my feet won't see holes,

I won't feel cold in my Performance Leather,

Like those with their toes exposed in cold weather,

My EVA filler with Bouncing Soles give me so much pleasure,

At work or at leisure,

My DM's can make me smart smooth rude cool or clever,

I treat them like a baby taking the utmost coochy-coo care,

Had the Gucci shoe even had the Nike Air,

But nothing can compare,

To my Dr. Martens Airwair.

By Prince Harrison, 2000

Bibliography

Books

Arnold, Gina
Route 666: On The Road To Nirvana
St Martin's Press Inc., 1993

Barnes, Richard
Mods!
Plexus, 1979

Brown, Gareth
Scooter Boys
Omnibus Press, 1996

Cross, Alan
The Alternative Music Almanac
Collector's Guide Publishing Inc., 1995

Daly, Steven and Nathaniel Wice
Alt.Culture: An A-Z of the '90s
Fourth Estate Ltd., 1995

De La Haye, Amy & Cathie Dingwall
Surfers, Soulies, Skinheads & Skaters
Victoria & Albert Museum, 1996

Earle, Fiona and Alan Dearling, Helen Whittle, Roddy Glasse and Gubby
A Time To Travel
Enabler Publications, 1994

Gimarc, George
Punk Diary 1970–1979
Vintage, 1994

Glennon, Lorraine, ed.
Our Time: The Illustrated History of the 20th Century
Turner Publishing Inc., 1995

Hebdige, Dick
Subculture - The Meaning of Style
Routledge, 1979

Horx, Matthias & Peter Wippermann, eds.
Markenkult
Trendburo, 1995

Jones, Dylan
Haircults
Thames & Hudson, 1990

Knight, Nick
Skinhead
Omnibus Press, 1982

Lazell, Barry
Punk! An A–Z
Hamlyn, 1995

McAleer, Dave
The All Music Book of Hit Albums
Miller Freeman Books, 1995

McAleer, Dave
The All Music Book of Hit Singles
Miller Freeman Books, 1994

McDowell, Colin
Shoes, Fashion and Fantasy
Thames & Hudson, 1989

McGartland, Tony
Buzzcocks: The Complete History
Independent Music Press, 1995

Marsh, Dave & James Bernard
The New Book of Rock Lists
Sidgwick & Jackson, 1994

Marshall, George
Spirit of '69: A Skinhead Bible
ST Publishing, 1991

Marshall, George
The Two Tone Story
ST Publishing, 1990

Marshall, George
Total Madness
ST Publishing, 1993

Mercer, Mick
The Gothic Rock Black Book
Omnibus Press, 1988

Morris, Desmond
The Soccer Tribe
Jonathan Cape, 1981

**Obstfeld, Raymond &
Patricia Fitzgerald**
Jabberock
Canongate Books Ltd, 1997

O'Keefe, Linda
*Shoes: A Celebration of Pumps,
Sandals, Slippers and More*
Workman Publishing, 1996

O'Regan, Denis
Images of Punk
Castle Communications Plc.,
1996

Owen, Jane
Camden Girls
Penguin, 1997

**Pattison, Angela & Nigel
Cawthorne**
*A Century of Shoes: Icons of
Style in the 20th Century*
Page One Pub. Pte. Ltd, 1997

Polhemus, Ted
Street Style
Thames & Hudson, 1994

Roach, Martin & The Prodigy
Prodigy: The Fat of the Land
Independent Music Press, 1997

Roach, Martin
*The Eight Legged Atomic
Dustbin Will Eat Itself*
Independent Music Press, 1992

Savage, Jon
England's Dreaming
Faber & Faber, 1991

Skarface, Fred
Our Culture
[publisher and date
of publication unknown]

Skarface, Fred
Tribes of England
[publisher and date
of publication unknown]

Storry, Mike & Peter Childs, eds.
British Cultural Identities
Routledge, 1997

Tobler, John, ed.
The NME Rock 'n' Roll Years
Reed International Books Ltd,
1990

Trasko, Mary
*Heavenly Soles: Extraordinary
20th Century Shoes*
Abbeville Press, USA, 1992

Tremlett, George
Slade
Futura Publications Ltd, 1975

Watson, Gavin
Skins
ST Publishing, 1994

Williams, Paul
*You're Wondering Now:
A History of The Specials*
ST Publishing, 1995

**eds. of *Rolling Stone*
magazine**
*Rolling Stone: Images of Rock &
Roll*
Little, Brown, 1995

Articles

Ackerman, Dan
'The Good Life – Report From
Boot Camp'
[Unknown publication]

Barnes, Richard
Sleeve liner notes for *The Who –
Who's Better, Who's Best*

Black, Johnny
'Eyewitness'
Q magazine, July 1996
Article on the first Glastonbury
Festival.

Boullemier, Tony
'Just What the Doctor Ordered'
Commerce magazine, February
1994

Dowey, Mary
Article on Dr Martens in Aer
Lingus' in-flight magazine, 1993

Ferguson, James
'A Brief Shoe History'
Financial Times, 31/10/87

Gaskell, Judith
Article in *Shoe & Leather News*,
4/1/85

Hill, Dave
Article in *City Limits*
19–25/10/84

Jacobs, Ulla
'Objects of Desire'
Weiner magazine, November
1992

Jourdan, Thea
Article in *The Scotsman*, 6/4/96

Lyons, Kate
Article in *Ragtrader*, 15/2/94

Mulholland, Neil
Article in *Sunday Life*, 20/6/93

Payne, Cindi
Article and interview with Dr
Klaus Maertens
Daily Mail, 20/2/85

Smith, Andrew
'The Death of Tribes'
Q magazine, November 1997

Spencer, Neil
Article on Dr Martens
The Face, April 1986

Thorne, Tony
'Fifty Years of Fashions, Fads
and Cults'
Daily Mail, 17/3/93

Tredre, Roger
Article in the *Independent*,
12/9/92

The following publications and
magazines have also proved
invaluable: *NME, Melody Maker,
Record Collector, Q, Vox, Select,
Rolling Stone, Oz Magazine,
Times, Daily Mail, Daily Express,
The Face, Loaded, What's Up
Doc, Footwear, Alternative
Press, Shoe & Leather News.*
Also the Airwair Archive and
Northampton Shoe Museum
Archive.

Dr. Martens on the Web

www.drmartens.com.

Acknowledgements

The author would like to thank:
Wayne Hemingway, for providing the foreword to this book. And everyone else who helped in the writing of this book.

Madness – *The Business* CD sleeve appears courtesy of Virgin Records.

'I Pay homage to Docs' is from http://magenta.com/~jetgrrl/toothpick/1star/drmarten.html

Every effort has been made to source and to credit fully and appropriately all material used in this book. Should any errors be contained therein, the author and publishers would be grateful to receive notification.

Picture credits

The publisher wishes to thank the organizations listed below for their kind permission to reproduce the photographs in this book. Every effort has been made to acknowledge the pictures, however we apologize if there are any unintentional omissions.

B = bottom; L = left; R = right; T = top.

Chrysalis Images /Neil Sutherland front cover, 2, 22, 36, 37, 39, 41, 43, 47, 55, /Michael Wicks 69, 70, 77, 87, 95, 103, 109, 117, 123, 131, 139, 153, 161, 169, 177, 185, 193, 201, 209, 217, 225, 241, 242, 249, 259, 290, 293.

Corbis 81TR, 127, 135TL, 144, 149TR, 159, 165, 166TC, 175, 191, 212, 215TL, 215TC, 215B, 231, 235TL, 235TR, 235B, 252, 255, 256, 268, /Neil Preston 74, 125, 198.

Digital Vision 113TL.

Dr. Martens back cover, 1, 6R, 11, 13, 15, 16, 18-19, 21, 25, 26-27, 32, 57, 58-59, 120, 143, 156, 194, 228, 233, 239.

Getty Images 29, 31TL, 31TR, 31B, 35, 44TL, 44CL, 44BL, 44R, 67, 81TL, 81TC, 81B, 88, 91, 132, 197.

Grade Design Consultants 171, 227, 285TR.

The Kobal Collection 101, 172, /Curbishley-Baird 155, /Paramount 135R, 135BL, 135CL, /RBT Stigwood Prods/Hemdale 65, /Warner Bros 97.

Martin Hampton 205.

Martin Roach/IMP Books 6L, 243.

PYMCA /© Richard Braine 79, 114, 118TL, 118R, /© Simon Buckle 283, /© Tom Oldham 277, /© Peter Francis 66, /© Derek Ridgers 48BC, 52, 118BL, 140, 150, /© Matt Smith 275, /© David Swindells 188, 260, /© Gavin Watson 48TR, 48BL, 48BR, 51, 60, 63, 98, 136.

Red Or Dead/Wayne Hemingway 219, 223.

Redferns Music Picture Library /George Chin 267, /Ian Dickson 85CL, /Mick Gold 107, Mick Hutson 272, 278, /Peter Pakvis 129.

Rex 31TC, 48TL, 73, 85TL, 85R, 85BL, 92, 100, 104, 110, 113TC, 113TR, 113B, 126, 137, 145, 147, 149TL, 149TC, 149B, 162, 166TL, 166TR, 166B, 178, 182, 187, 203, 206, 211, 215TR, 221, 235TC, 236, 245, 246, 251, 263, 265, 271, 281, 285TL, 285TC, 285B, 286, 289, 294, 297.

ST Publishing /from Skinhead Bible 82.

Virgin Records /Madness CD sleeve appears courtesy of Virgin Records 181.